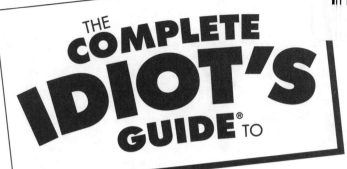

THE COMPLETE **IDIOT'S** GUIDE® TO

Jams, Jellies, and Preserves

by Yvonne Tremblay

ALPHA

A member of Penguin Group (USA) Inc.

To my grandmother, Margaret Susan Stefan, whose kitchen was a source of warmth for body and soul and of good things to eat.

International Standard Book Number: 0-02-864486-7
Library of Congress Catalog Card Number: 2003100691

05   04   03   8   7   6   5   4   3   2   1

Interpretation of the printing code: The rightmost number of the first series of numbers is the year of the book's printing; the rightmost number of the second series of numbers is the number of the book's printing. For example, a printing code of 03-1 shows that the first printing occurred in 2003.

Printed in the United States of America

Note: This publication contains the opinions and ideas of its author. It is intended to provide helpful and informative material on the subject matter covered. It is sold with the understanding that the author and publisher are not engaged in rendering professional services in the book. If the reader requires personal assistance or advice, a competent professional should be consulted.

The author and publisher specifically disclaim any responsibility for any liability, loss, or risk, personal or otherwise, which is incurred as a consequence, directly or indirectly, of the use and application of any of the contents of this book.

Most Alpha books are available at special quantity discounts for bulk purchases for sales promotions, premiums, fund-raising, or educational use. Special books, or book excerpts, can also be created to fit specific needs.

For details, write: Special Markets, Alpha Books, 375 Hudson Street, New York, NY 10014.

Publisher: *Marie Butler-Knight*
Product Manager: *Phil Kitchel*
Senior Managing Editor: *Jennifer Chisholm*
Senior Acquisitions Editor: *Renee Wilmeth*
Development Editor: *Nancy D. Lewis*
Senior Production Editor: *Christy Wagner*
Copy Editor: *Jan Zunkel*
Illustrator: *Chris Eliopoulos*
Cover/Book Designer: *Trina Wurst*
Indexer: *Brad Herriman*
Layout/Proofreading: *Mary Hunt, Ayanna Lacey*

Contents at a Glance

Contents

10 Fruit Butters   191

11 Chutneys   205

Introduction

Creating this book has given me the opportunity to do what I love most—play in the kitchen. I was one of those kids who made mud and snow pies on the neighbors' steps. My friend had an Easy Bake Oven, and I wanted one—I was fascinated by the delicious-smelling cakes that came out of the tiny pans. My mom said that if I wanted to cook, I could bake big cakes in a real oven. I come from a big family, with four brothers and a sister, so I got a lot of hands-on experience in the kitchen.

I grew up in Thunder Bay, Ontario, but spent many summers on my grandparents' southern Saskatchewan farm, where there was an abundance of fresh eggs and milk and garden-grown vegetables. I churned butter, baked homemade bread, and canned fruit with my grandmother. It is where I grew to love cooking.

I attended the University of Guelph, Ontario, graduating with a degree in Applied Science in Food and Nutrition. It has always been my belief that the bridge between nutrition and healthy eating is in making healthy food taste good. For the past 10 years, I have made my living as a freelance food consultant doing just that.

Just for fun, in 1994, I decided to enter the Royal Agricultural Winter Fair in Toronto, Ontario, in the Jams and Jellies competition, to take my wares to my local fair (the "Royal" began in 1922 and is a prestigious event). I had two entries and was pleasantly surprised to win first prize for my Apple Cider Rosemary Jelly (it's in the book!). I have returned every year except one, entering all the categories (only one entry is allowed per category) and have been honored with the title of Grand Champion Jam and Jelly Maker three times (highest overall points). My friends and family just call me "Jelly Queen"—long may she jam!

When I was asked to write *Prizewinning Preserves*, from which this book is based, I had not entered enough recipes into competition to fill a book. Therefore, I asked a number of my co-competitors at the Royal to join me in sharing prized and prize-winning recipes. I have so enjoyed speaking with each one of them, learning how they first got into preserving, what they like making most, and so on. Some are men and some are women; some pick wild berries; some sell their products; some do it as a hobby and for gift-giving. I count myself in good company and am thrilled to include their wonderful recipes (all were tested for the book). For their names, please see the acknowledgments.

I spent the summer of 2000 making delicious preserves of almost any kind you can imagine. Believe it or not, I am not tired of it. I have never been so sticky or had so much fun. I have included all-time favorites and added twists and turns to come up with interesting new tastes, too. You're gonna love 'em! My official tasters (my friends and family) guarantee it.

How This Book Is Organized

This book is divided into two parts:

Part 1, "Getting Started (Primer on Preserving)," brings you up to date on the latest canning and food safety guidelines, reviews the basics of jam- and jelly-making, and gives you expert tips for prizewinning results, whether this is a new experience or you are a seasoned pro. A recommended equipment list, an altitude chart for processing times, and a word on fruit and pectins will start you on the road to skillful mastery of the art (and science) of jam-making (jelly-making, conserve-making, and so on).

Part 2, "The Recipes," is one of the most extensive collections of sweet preserves available today. There are 55 recipes for jams alone, using almost any fruit you can think of. Preserving might have basic instructions, but there is nothing plain and simple about the taste! You're going to learn how to make *great* jams, jellies, marmalades, and more! The final two chapters contain delicious recipes for desserts and dishes you can make using your preserves.

Extra Bites

The sidebars in this book offer tips, inspiration, valuable knowledge, and definitions.

 Well Defined
Definitions of key terms or cooking methods you will need to know in order to easily understand what to do.

 Fruitful Trivia
Useful and informative stuff to know about fruit and tips for preparation, handling, and storage.

 Fast Lane
Tips for speeding up your work so you can quickly move through the recipes.

 Word to the Wise
Cautionary advice about common pitfalls, dangers, and obsolete canning procedures.

Acknowledgments

Two special people helped me create this book.

The first is Patricia Moynihan-Morris, a dear friend and food consultant. Pat helped me test a lot of the recipes and was always cheerful, even when painstakingly slicing citrus peel for marmalade and cutting up fresh pineapple. Some days it felt like a factory assembly line: chopping fruit, measuring sugar, stirring, sterilizing, bottling, processing, labeling, and storing. Pat was also great with feedback, tasting expertise, and moral support.

The second person who played a major role was my friend Lise Ferguson, who entered and edited recipes, helping me find just the right words to explain how to do what is second nature to me. She makes food writers out of cooks (and, like me, believes that angels come to help along the way). Extra special thanks for coming to the rescue once again when I needed help with transforming *Prizewinning Preserves* into a *Complete Idiot's Guide*. You are always a complete angel and are irreplaceable.

Thank you to my family members, among whom are many fine cooks. You have always cheered me on and shared the excitement of my wins and successes. Thank you to my friends, especially Sandra, Sonja, Judy, Luisa, Micki, Wendi, and Rose, who are there for me in all of life's challenges and who keep telling me that I make the best jam in the world.

Thank you to Nicole de Montbrun, acquisitions editor at Prentice Hall, for coming up with the idea and giving me the opportunity to do my first cookbook, *Prizewinning Preserves*. Her enthusiasm about the preserves and accolades upon tasting some of them kept me going as the summer wore on. My gratitude also for her assistance in the *Complete Idiot's Guide* opportunity and for our ongoing friendship. Many thanks to Renee Wilmeth, senior acquisitions editor for Alpha Books, who has given me the chance to have this book join the *Complete Idiot's Guide* cooking series, which help people discover the fun and accomplishment of cooking.

I am grateful to my fellow and lady jam (and other preserves) makers for allowing me to include some of their prizewinning pursuits in this book: Paul Barrie of East York, Ontario, who was 1995 Grand Champion at the Royal Agricultural Winter Fair in Toronto, Ontario, and who is teaching his son his tricks; Larry McGuire of Hamilton, Ontario, who holds preserving bees with friends who have become addicted to his preserves; Gayle Rowan of Haliburton, Ontario, who follows her own path to the woods to pick wild berries for jams she sells under the name Wolfpath Products; Barbara Mander of Mississauga, Ontario, who loves to give her jams in gift baskets; Sharon Evans of Haliburton, Ontario, whose preserves grace the tables of cottage country B&Bs; and Shirley McMurray of Stoney Creek, Ontario, who sells her jellies in the Niagara region under the name The Jelly Crate (Shirley has a special outfit she wears when preserving—black leggings, a long black T-shirt, old running shoes, and a cap). The love of jamming they have shared is inspiring and comes through in their jams, jellies, and other sweet preserves.

I would like to thank the companies who support us all in our preserving endeavors: Alltrista Corporation (who supplies jars, lids, pectin products, and canning equipment) and Kraft Foods, Inc. (makers of liquid and powdered fruit pectins) for their commitment, their expertise, and the contribution of a few of their recipes.

Hats off to the farmers who grow the quality fruit that is the basis for exquisite preserves.

Last, thank you for taking this book home with you. The fun is about to begin!

Trademarks

All terms mentioned in this book that are known to be or are suspected of being trademarks or service marks have been appropriately capitalized. Alpha Books and Penguin Group (USA) Inc. cannot attest to the accuracy of this information. Use of a term in this book should not be regarded as affecting the validity of any trademark or service mark.

Part 1

Getting Started
(Primer on Preserving)

Preserving of any kind can seem a daunting undertaking. There is an issue of food safety, and it can seem like such a labor-intensive event. In Part 1, you will learn the most up-to-date preserving information, what equipment is needed to get started, how to prepare and preserve to get it "right," how to test for doneness, as well as terms and tips to achieve prizewinning results. What's great about preserving is that once you learn it, it's pretty much the same procedure for all the preserves in this book.

Choosing and preparing the fruit is also an important part of achieving excellent flavor for your jams, jellies, and other preserves. Information is provided for various types of fruit as well as the levels of pectin found in specific types of fruit and commercial pectins.

A Primer on Preserving

In This Chapter

- Everything you need to know to get you up and running (you can do this!)
- Necessary and helpful equipment to have
- Importance of food safety, with the most up-to-date info
- Inside tips to get expert results

This is where it all begins. What you will learn here will provide the base for making all of the preserve recipes in this book. If you are new to this skill, you will learn the right steps from the beginning to become proficient. If you are a veteran preserver, then this will be a good update and review of the latest preserving information. Here you will learn everything you need to know to get high-quality results and perhaps improve upon your skills.

This chapter provides some useful and necessary information to help you succeed at making top-quality sweet preserves that will keep well.

Learn about the importance of food safety, the nutrition of preserves, what equipment is necessary or helpful to make each of the recipes, tips on where to find equipment and utensils.

As you prepare yourself to start, I will take you through the proper procedures for sterilizing jars and equipment, preparation of lids and boiling water processing. This will help you to be successful in preserving your jams, jellies, etc. so they will not spoil in storage. You sure don't want to go to all the time, expense of ingredients, and trouble then have product that does not keep. A chart is included for additional times for altitude.

I will tell you about several tests for determining the setting point (how to tell when the preserve is done).

Most critical are the tips that will help you make excellent quality preserves—with great color, flavor, and texture.

Food Safety

When making preserves, keeping things sanitary is most important. Microbes—usually molds, yeasts, and bacteria—are responsible for food spoilage. Spoilage ruins the flavor and consistency of preserves; more important, some toxins produced by the microbes can be lethal. It is never worth the risk to consume suspect food; discard food that has been kept too long, in which you can see moving bubbles, for which the seal has broken, or where there is obvious mold growth.

The high concentration of sugar found in jams, jellies, and other sweet preserves is responsible for deterring the growth of molds. But molds will grow on the surface, as well as inside the preserve, in the presence of air. That is why processing is recommended, to provide an airtight seal and to kill any organisms that may get into the jar from utensils or the air during filling. Processing is even more important for low-sugar preserves or nonsugar spreads. Preserves may also be frozen, without processing, for safe long-term storage.

Nutrition

Although preserves are generally high in sugar, they contain virtually no fat. Butter and margarine have about 100 kcal (calories) and 11 g of fat per tablespoon. The same amount of most regular jams contains about 55 kcal and no fat, while no-sugar (artificially sweetened or no-sugar-added) spreads range from 10 to 15 kcal per tablespoon. Jams made with light pectin crystals have 20 percent less sugar and 30 percent more fruit. Preserves contain no protein and are primarily carbohydrate from the fruit and the sugar.

Remember that preserves retain a lot of the nutrients that were present in the fruit. Some of the vitamins are destroyed by heat and exposure to air when the fruit is cut; however, many vitamins, minerals, and phytochemicals (plant compounds thought to be beneficial in prevention of certain diseases) are retained. Preserves often contain the seeds and peels of fruits, which are good sources of fiber, as is the flesh itself. Pectin is a type of soluble fiber.

Preserves can be part of your nutritious eating, especially when you eat them on whole-grain breads (complex carbohydrates) that are also rich in fiber. Whole grains help slow down the absorption of sugars (simple carbohydrates) into the bloodstream, which can be beneficial for those with blood-sugar problems. Eating simple carbohydrates with proteins works as well—try a little jam stirred into plain yogurt to sweeten.

Of course, don't overdo it. Excess calories (calories over and above our energy needs) will all be converted to and stored as fat, no matter what foods they come from.

Equipment

This section will give you an idea of the types of equipment you will need for preserving. Some items are regular kitchen equipment, others are specific to canning or while not essential will help to make the job easier. You don't need to spend a lot to get started. With this book to help, I know you will enjoy canning, so why not make the investment as you will want to make more preserves after your first success! Tools make the job a lot easier and quicker. Trust me on that.

- ◆ **Large, heavy-bottomed pot.** Thin-bottomed pots will likely cause scorching, and pots that are too small will result in messy boil-overs. Most sets of cooking pots include a large, wide pot or Dutch oven with a lid. Other large pots, such as stock pots, may also be suitable. The bottom of the pot should have an extra layer of metal; it is usually aluminum or copper, which are good heat conductors. Do not use all-aluminum or all-iron pots.

Word to the Wise _____

I like to use wide-mouth pots for jams, butters, marmalades, conserves, and chutneys. They allow for greater evaporation of water when you are cooking down the mixture to thicken it. I have another pot that is taller and a little narrower in which I prefer to make jellies. The jelly liquid often bubbles up high and could overflow a shorter pot. You need a pot with a depth at least four times that of the liquid.

- **Large kettle.** Any large pot is good for sterilizing jars and for processing the preserves. For processing, the pot must be deep enough to allow water to cover jars by at least one inch.

- **Small saucepan.** This is used to boil jar lids to soften the sealing compound.

- **Bowls.** Large and small bowls are used for pre-measured fruit, dried fruit, sugar, nuts, etc. Small glass plates or bowls can be placed in the freezer and used to check the setting point.

- **Knives.** You need a good quality chef's knife for chopping, and a paring knife for peeling and trimming. A knife sharpener keeps knives sharp so you can work faster and avoid cuts due to knife slipping.

- **Cutting boards.** Have a large plastic cutting board, with a groove to catch juices, for chopping citrus fruit, pineapple, peaches, and so on; also have a wooden board for cutting onions, peppers, garlic, etc. for chutney (do not use for fruit as the flavors will be transferred).

- **Other.** Food processor, food mill, colander, strainers, scale, plastic-coated apron.

Utensils

As it is important to measure properly, you will need a variety of measures for liquid and dry ingredients. Spoons are essential for stirring and skimming. For filling jars you will need a ladle and canning funnel. One of my most favorite and useful utensils is a tool called a magnetic wand, which is so handy for taking prepared metal lids out of the hot water. A bubble remover does just what it says—it removes trapped air, that can cause spoilage. Rubber spatulas and a potato masher are probably already among your basic kitchen tools. A good timer is important for timing accuracy so you get a good consistency and set (this is all rather a fun science project that you get to eat at the end!). A digital thermometer will help to determine setting point for non-pectin added preserves.

- **Measures.** Glass liquid measures, and metal or plastic measuring cups and spoons for dry measure, are needed for accurate measuring. Do not measure sugar in a liquid measure and do not measure liquids (water, juice, wine, and so on) in cups for dry measure. Fruit may be measured in either, although I prefer a 4 cup liquid measure for large quantities of fruit (once it is empty, use it for discarding skimmed material).

- **Spoons.** Wooden spoons are great for stirring, and ones with extra-long handles are ideal for avoiding hot splashes from bubbling preserves (I wrote "Magic

Wand" on the handle of one of mine). Mark wooden spoon handles so you do not interchange ones you use for sweet and savory preserves. Don't leave wooden spoons in your mixture to "cook": Remove after stirring. Plastic or melamine spoons are not as good for the constant stirring of hot mixtures. Use a metal spoon (stainless steel or chrome-plated) for skimming foam from the tops of jams and jellies.

◆ **Ladle.** I prefer a ladle (stainless-steel or chrome-plated) for transferring mixtures to jars.

◆ **Canning funnel.** Most of the ones available today are plastic. They make it easier to ladle preserves into jars.

◆ **Magnetic wand.** A magnet attached to the end of a plastic wand, this is a fairly recent invention that is handy for lifting prepared jar lids from hot water. You simply touch the magnet to the center of the metal lid, place the lid on top of the clean jar rim, and detach with your finger. These wands are not expensive, and are sold directly by Bernardin Ltd. if you cannot find them in a hardware or general merchandise store. (See Appendix B for more information.)

◆ **Bubble remover.** Alltrista Corp. sells a handy plastic tool called Ball Bubble FREER Spatula for removing bubbles from inside the jar. (See www. homecanning.com for more information.)

◆ **Rubber spatula/scraper.** This is used to scrape sugar from inside edges of the pot. Look for high-heat-resistant spatulas in upscale kitchen stores. A narrow spatula can be used to remove air bubbles.

◆ **Potato masher or pastry blender.** Use to crush fruit to release juices.

◆ **Kitchen timer.** A digital timer ensures accurate timing of boiling and cooking.

◆ **Candy or digital thermometer.** Use to test the temperature for setting point.

◆ **Other.** Cheesecloth, jelly bag, cherry pitter, strawberry huller, or wide drinking straw (to remove strawberry hulls and stems), vegetable peeler, citrus zester, graters, citrus juicer.

Fast Lane

Use a wide straw to quickly remove hulls and stems from strawberries. Simply position the straw on the pointed end of the strawberry and push upward toward the stem. The whole thing just pops out!

Where to Find Stuff

Hardware or general merchandise stores usually carry the full line of canning paraphernalia: jars, extra lids, magnetic wands, canning funnels, and jar lifters, extra labels, and so on. Many of these products, although not essential, do make canning easier

Fast Lane _____
Get yourself a plastic coated apron to protect your clothes and save yourself from doing extra laundry. If preserves splash while cooking or transferring to jars, they just wipe off with a damp cloth.

and are worth the small investment. I place spare lids and rings, funnels, and so on, in plastic storage bags to keep them clean and together when not in use.

Housewares sections of department and discount stores, specialty kitchen supplies stores, and supermarkets carry cookware, utensils, and gadgets. If you can, spend the extra money for quality goods.

You can purchase canning items online at www. homecanning.com.

Preserving with the Best Results

The following are tips for prizewinning results:

1. Always follow guidelines for food safety and sterilization of jars and utensils.

2. Use reliable recipes and measure carefully.

3. Always follow product instructions for commercial pectins and do not interchange liquid and powdered pectin in recipes.

4. Do not alter the amount of sugar, or your preserves may not set.

5. Select ingredients of the best quality. Picking your own fruit is a good way to obtain quality, as is buying from farmers' markets. The smell of the fruit will give you an idea of its flavor. Fruit should be fragrant and have good aroma of the particular fruit (for example, peaches should smell very peachy). Avoid overripe fruit; however, some slightly underripe fruit is actually good, as its natural pectin levels are usually higher. Because underripe fruit may be less juicy, do not use more than 25 percent underripe fruit.

6. Prepare fruits as outlined in the recipe: wash, stem, pit, peel, chop well, and so on. If peels are not normally *eaten* on a fruit—as in kiwi, mango, pineapple—then remove the peels. For fruits like peaches, peel them if the recipe tells you to; for fruits like apricots and plums, leave peels on. (For more details, see the "Fruit Information" section in Chapter 2.)

7. Time the cooking carefully, preferably using a digital timer, or use the second hand on a clock. Remove pot from stove immediately to stop the cooking. For preserves made without added commercial pectin, test for setting point or doneness at the minimum time given. If mixture has not set, return to heat, bring back to a boil, begin timing for another minute or two, and test again; repeat until ready. Do not overcook or your preserves will be gluey.

8. Certain preserves will benefit from five to seven minutes of stirring after being removed from the heat. This will prevent bits from floating to the top of the jar instead of being suspended throughout. Floating can occur when ingredients have not been chopped finely enough, as specified in the recipe. Peaches, pears, strawberries, and sweet peppers have a tendency to float.

9. Leave recommended space from the rim (headspace) when filling jars (specified in recipe).

10. Do not overtighten jar lids, before or after processing or after cooling.

11. Let jars rest upright at room temperature, undisturbed until set. *Do not invert jars.*

12. Remove rings and wipe away any stickiness, especially from jar threads and under rings. Store jars in a cool, dark, dry place. Use within one year for best quality.

Word to the Wise

Tightening jar rings after preserves have been processed or after they have cooled can disturb/weaken the seal. Once the lids invert and seal (vacuum pressure), the rings are no longer serving a purpose and can be removed altogether. I prefer to leave them on (after removing to wipe any stickiness) so they are with the jar after it is opened.

The Least You Need to Know

♦ Follow food safety practices religiously so that your preserves don't become contaminated and spoil; get familiar with the current recommendations.

♦ Don't interchange commercial pectin types because the recipes were developed with a specific pectin with gelling qualities in balance with the other ingredients. If you use the wrong pectin in the recipe it likely will not gel and as a result be a waste of ingredients and your precious time.

♦ Basic canning procedures are similar for jams, jellies, conserves, marmalades, fruit butters, and chutneys (with minor changes), so once you learn it, the same information applies.

Notes

_____

_____

_____

_____

_____

_____

_____

_____

_____

_____

_____

_____

_____

_____

_____

_____

_____

_____

_____

_____

_____

_____

_____

_____

_____

Notes

Chapter 2

Facts on Fruit

In This Chapter

- ◆ Choosing good-quality fruit
- ◆ Information on storing and freezing fruit
- ◆ Learning about pectin

The flavor and ripeness of the fruit you choose for preserving is critical to making good jams, jellies, and so on. If the fruit is the proper ripeness and void of any blemishes it will be fragrant and of excellent taste. If the fruit looks beautiful and smells appetizing, the resulting preserve will have the potential to be delicious. I choose the best I can find. If I cannot find what I'm looking for, I either wait or make something else. When you find great-quality fruit, freeze some for later use or for combination jams later in the season. Sometimes there is too much fruit to deal with at one time. Mother Nature and weather conditions can make a real jumble out of the seasonality of fruit, with several in season at the same time (so much fruit, so little time!).

Be meticulous in your handling and preparation of the fruit. Trim away bad spots, discard leaves, hulls, stems, and seeds (where not a part of the fruit, such as berries). Wash all fruit well (even though you are going to cook it) to eliminate any dirt, insecticides, or microbes. Use fruit when it is fresh rather then waiting/storing for several days. Make use of commercial frozen fruit as it is sometimes less expensive and has been cleaned for convenience (e.g., strawberries have been hulled and stemmed, peaches have been peeled and pitted, gooseberries have been bearded, currants have been stemmed and bearded). You can often find out of season fruit as well. Winter is a great time for preserving.

Fruit Information

Use only good-quality, blemish-free fruit; trim away bad spots. To hasten ripening of some fruit (for example, peaches, pears, and mangoes), place in a paper bag at room temperature.

Fruitful Trivia

To prevent browning and flavor-loss of fruit, use Fruit-Fresh, an antioxidant manufactured by Alltrista Corp. (See Appendix B for this and other useful websites.)

Word to the Wise

Use only frozen fruit that has not had sugar added to it, as it will throw off the balance in the recipe and it may not set as well and be too sweet.

Store firm, ripe fruit in a cool place to prevent deterioration, and use it quickly. Store berries (except cranberries) in a single layer under a paper towel in the refrigerator. Most other fruit should be kept in plastic bags in the crisper drawer. Handle tender fruits delicately to avoid bruising.

I usually freeze rhubarb, currants, and most berries to have on hand (when out of season) to make combination fruit preserves. I prefer to use tree fruit fresh in season when it is abundant and less expensive, and prefer not to freeze it. However, packaged frozen fruit is perfectly fine for making preserves. *Note:* For accuracy, measure fruit that has been partially thawed (is still partially frozen).

All fruit needs to be washed, rinsed, and drained, preferably just before using.

Here is a listing of many of the fruits used in jams, jellies, and preserves:

♦ **Apples.** Apples are used in a lot of preserves and are available year round. One large apple yields about 1 cup chopped. For jams and butters, choose apples that lose their shape and soften when cooked: McIntosh, Cortland, Empire, or Russet. For conserves and chutneys, choose apples that keep their shape when cooked: Golden Delicious, Jonagold, Crispin (Mutsu), Idared, Spy, or Spartan. Sometimes a combination of both can be used. Apples are peeled and cored; for fruit butters, the peel is left on, and the stem and blossom ends are removed. Older, less crisp apples are great for making butters. Crabapples make excellent jelly. Red Delicious apples are not recommended for cooking. *Do not freeze apples* *for preserving as they have to be frozen with sugar.* That is suitable for pies, but not suitable for the preserves in this book. They brown easily as well. Apples are available in the supermarket pretty much year round and I prefer to use them fresh for preserving.

♦ **Apricots.** Choose firm, ripe, or slightly under-ripe fruit. Do not peel; discard pit. Dried apricots have good flavor and are used to make fruit butters, or are added to conserves and chutneys. *Do not use frozen apricots for preserving as they require added juice, sugar, or syrup.* They also need to have the skins removed and when you make preserves you want to use the skin as it adds color, flavor and texture to jams and conserves.

♦ **Berries.** Choose firm, ripe, dry fruit. Fresh or frozen berries can be used; frozen berries will produce more juice when thawed, so preserves may need slightly more cooking time. Do not store fresh berries too long before using. Remove hull and stems from strawberries after washing. Boysenberries are a raspberry/blackberry/loganberry cross. There are many regional berries that are terrific for preserves and may be substituted in recipes. *To freeze:* Wash and dry well on paper towel; lay whole berries in single layer on baking sheet; freeze completely; then transfer to freezer bags or containers.

♦ **Cherries.** Choose firm, ripe, glossy fruit. Store in refrigerator. Remove stems and pits. Use cherry-pitter, or halve fruit and remove pit with paring knife. May be frozen after pitting, like berries. Sweet or tart cherries may be used to make jams and conserves; use tart cherries for jelly. You may find that purchasing commercial prepared frozen, pitted cherries will save you a lot of time.

♦ **Citrus fruit (oranges, grapefruit, lemons, limes).** Choose firm, deep-colored, glossy fruit with blemish-free rinds that are heavy for their size. Store in refrigerator; freeze extra juice in ice-cube trays, then transfer to freezer bags. Before using for marmalades, scrub rind well with soapy water and rinse. *Do not freeze citrus fruit for preserving.*

♦ **Currants.** Red and black currants are great for jams or jellies. Choose firm, ripe, dry fruit. Remove from stems; black currants need blossom ends snipped for jams (not necessary for jelly). Freeze like berries.

♦ **Cranberries.** Choose firm, ripe, red fruit. Freeze when in season; place bags of whole berries inside a freezer bag to prevent them from drying out (or transfer to plastic freezer container); then put directly into freezer.

♦ **Gooseberries.** Choose firm, brightly colored fruit, when green or when ripe (red or purple). Remove "beards" by snipping off blossom ends. Freeze like berries.

- **Grapes.** Concord grapes are the most popular; choose firm, not soft. Remove stems before cooking. Use whole for making juice for jelly. *Do not freeze Concord grapes for preserving.*

- **Kiwifruit.** Choose firm, ripe fruit. Always peel. *Do not freeze kiwifruit for preserving as they require added juice, sugar, or syrup.*

- **Mangoes.** Choose firm, ripe fruit (gives slightly when pressed) that is fragrant. Can be ripened at home. Always peel and remove pit; slice on each side of pit; then remove flesh around pit and inside slices. *Do not freeze mangoes for preserving as they require added juice, sugar or syrup.*

- **Nectarines.** Choose firm, ripe, or slightly underripe fruit (but without green areas). Do not peel; remove pit. *Do not freeze nectarines for preserving as they require added juice, sugar, or syrup.*

- **Papayas.** Choose fruit with smooth, wrinkle-free skin. Can be ripened at home at room temperature; it's ripe when fruit gives slightly when pressed. Will keep in refrigerator several days after ripening. Peel and remove seeds. *Do not freeze papaya for preserving as they require added juice, sugar, or syrup.*

- **Peaches.** Choose firm, ripe, or slightly underripe fruit (but without green areas). Peel and remove pit before using. *Do not freeze peaches for preserving as they require added juice, sugar, or syrup.*

- **Pears.** Always picked underripe; ripen at home before using. Always peel (except for use in butters) and core. *Do not freeze pears, the texture becomes mushy.*

- **Plums.** Choose firm, ripe, or slightly underripe fruit. Do not peel. Pit not always removed before cooking; e.g., for Damson Plum Jam, pits are removed while cooking. *Do not freeze plums for preserving as they require added juice, sugar, or syrup.*

- **Pineapple.** Choose one that is sweet and fragrant with nice green leaves. Extra-sweet varieties are now available. Slice off top and bottom, stand on end, pare off skin in lengthwise pieces, remove eyes, quarter, and remove core. A good serrated knife makes removing skin a lot easier. *Do not freeze pineapple for preserving as it requires added juice, water, or syrup.*

- **Rhubarb.** Choose firm stalks that are not too large (large stalks become woody). Usually cut into half-size or smaller pieces. *To freeze:* Place chopped pieces in plastic freezer bag or container.

Understanding Fruit's Natural Pectin

Pectin is a type of soluble fiber and is highest in and under the skin of fruit, as well as in the seeds and flesh. Pectin, sugar, and high acidity are necessary for the gelling of preserves. Some fruit have abundant natural pectin, and do not require additional pectin to be added and do not need to be cooked very long before they will set. Fruit lower in pectin must be cooked down to evaporate water and concentrate the pectin. High-pectin fruit can be combined with fruit that is lower in pectin to assist in gelling.

Commercial pectins are extracted from citrus fruit and are great for providing Mother Nature with a boost. Some preserves cannot be made without added commercial pectin (some fruit is too low in its own natural pectin), while some recipes include added pectin for ease, quickness of cooking, and as an aid for those who may have trouble determining setting point. Pectin-added recipes often give a higher yield than ones where the fruit is cooked down a lot. The recipes in this book have it all worked out for you, so not to worry!

These are fruits that are naturally high in pectin:

- Tart apples (crabapples)
- Citrus fruit (Seville oranges, grapefruit, lemons, limes)
- Cranberries
- Red and black currants
- Gooseberries
- Concord grapes
- Sour plums (Damson)
- Quinces

Fast Lane
Look for commercial pectins in the section where they keep the canning jars and equipment. It is quickest to ask the staff where they are located, as it could be anywhere in the store and might not be at all easy to find.

These are fruits with moderate levels of pectin:

- Sweeter apples (McIntosh, Golden Delicious, and so on)
- Blackberries
- Boysenberries
- Sour and sweet cherries
- Elderberries
- Grapes

Word to the Wise

Do not double recipes. Your pot may overflow, even if it does not look that full. Also, cooking in too large a quantity may cause fruit to become overcooked or prevent thickening/gelling.

- Guavas
- Kiwis
- Loganberries
- Melons
- Sweet oranges
- Sweet plums
- Raspberries

Other fruits will all have some pectin in low amounts. Under-ripe fruit is higher in pectin and may be used in some preserves.

The Least You Need to Know

- Always choose high-quality fruit that is fragrant and ripe. Prepare carefully (ensure that it is washed) by trimming away bad spots and blemishes.
- Berries, cherries, currants, gooseberries, and rhubarb are easily frozen for preserving.
- Don't interchange commercial pectin types, or the recipe may not work.

Notes

Notes

Part 2

The Recipes

There are approximately 130 recipes and variations in this book for jams, jellies, conserves, marmalades, fruit butters, and chutneys using single fruits as well as amazing fruit combinations. These are the best of the best, most having captured top prizes in fair competitions. All recipes are in small batches so you don't have to spend all day in the kitchen. You can make your preserves in stages, too, measuring sugar and assembling equipment the day before. You will be surprised how easy it really is! Follow the recipes in this part religiously, and you will have success.

There are also 20 recipes for using your preserves as ingredients—including my favorite recipe for preserves on fresh baked scones.

Chapter 3

Fabulous Fruit Jams

In This Chapter

- ◆ What is a jam and how not to get into one
- ◆ Tips for expert ease with jams
- ◆ How to prevent floating fruit
- ◆ What to do to prevent or fix errors

Jams are spreads made from one or more fruit, crushed or chopped, combined with sugar or sugar substitute, cooked or uncooked, and set by naturally present pectin or commercial pectin, with a thick, spreadable consistency.

Jams range from simple, one-fruit-and-sugar mixtures to multiple fruit medleys, and mixtures with spices or added liqueurs. We all seem to have favorites, some personally appealing flavor that we savor on scones, English muffins, grainy breads, or bagels. Maybe your favorite is something your mother or grandmother made that has special memories associated with it. Maybe it is something you picked up at a fair or market. Whatever your fancy, there is nothing like the fresh, unique flavor of homemade jam.

This collection features jams made with and without added pectin, and includes some no-cook, low-sugar, and no-sugar recipes. Some people find it easier to make jams with added liquid pectin or crystals because the cooking time is shorter and does not require testing for setting point. Even easier are the no-cook jams, which do not require sterilization and processing.

Pectin Perfection

Commercial pectins are very useful for jam- and jelly-making. They were originally developed as a powdered fruit pectin. Now liquid fruit pectin is also available. When added to fruit that is low in natural pectin, they allow it to gel without having to cook it excessively. As a jam cooks the naturally present pectin would eventually concentrate and thicken the jam. However, lengthy cooking can diminish the fresh fruit flavor and darken or change the color. There is a tendency to overcook it as well and end up with a product that is too thick and gluey or too sweet in taste.

Jams made with commercial pectin require more sugar but give a greater yield for the amount of fruit used. Commercial pectins are natural fruit pectins, extracted from apples or the peel of citrus fruit. They give Mother Nature a helping hand.

Commercial pectins come with recipes (see the leaflet inside the box) for most basic types of jam: strawberry, raspberry, peach, and so on. Commercial pectins are used for no-cook jams, helping them to retain vivid color and fresh-picked flavor and for no-sugar jams.

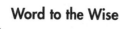 **Word to the Wise**

Do not interchange liquid and powdered pectin in recipes because these two types of pectins each have different gelling qualities as well as methods for use (for example, when they are added to the fruit and how long they are cooked after adding). Recipes are developed using a specific type, in the proper balance with the sugar and the acid and may not work if interchanged.

Jammin' Fun

Many of the recipes here are brand-new creations, interesting combinations never before tried. They have been designed to be as easy to make as possible. I have made as many as six jams in one day, so for you to make one should be no problem. Jam making can be done in stages: assembling ingredients, measuring sugar the day before, washing jars ahead, and so on. Once you get organized, it goes very well.

I developed the recipes specifically to have small yields so that you don't have to prepare too much fruit at one time. After all, even if you like to cook, you don't want to be in the kitchen all day. With a smaller yield, you can try a jam and see if you like it, or make a variety of different ones to have on hand or to give as gifts.

Word to the Wise

Please review Chapter 1 to reacquaint yourself with preserve-making. Things may have changed since you first started making preserves. If you are a beginner, there are a few important things to know before getting started. Many instructions are common to all preserves so, once you get it right for one, you'll sail through the others. It's a lot easier than you might think.

Testing, One, Two ...

Jams were tested for sugar content using a refractometer, so no more sugar was added than was needed for a good set. A refractometer has a delicate prism inside of it. A little of the preserve is placed on its small glass surface. It is held up to the light, and when you look through the eye piece (looks like a six-inch telescope), the percentage of sugar present shows up on a scale.

Acidity was also tested with a pH meter to ensure sufficient acid for gelling.

Tips for Prizewinning Jams

Stop here before beginning to cook for tips on how to get expert results:

◆ Choose top-quality, firm, ripe fruit. Up to 25 percent underripe fruit can be used when making non-pectin-added jams, as it is higher in pectin than ripe fruit. Be meticulous in your preparation of the fruit. Trim any bad spots or blemishes; chop thoroughly and slice evenly.

◆ Measure carefully. When adding the sugar, stir well to ensure that it is completely dissolved, scraping down any that gets on the sides of the pot or spoon handle. Undissolved sugar can crystallize in your jam. Heating the fruit a little before stirring in the sugar will help the sugar to dissolve more quickly.

◆ Stir and watch your jam; pectin-added jams require a full boil, constantly stirred. Simmered jams with natural pectin will thicken as they cook; reduce temperature and stir more often to prevent scorching.

◆ The timing for pectin-added jams should be exact, so use a timer. Check expiration date on the box of pectin before beginning. Do not interchange liquid pectin and crystals in recipes. Mix in pectin well.

◆ For jams without added pectin, timing will vary depending on the moisture and natural sugars in the fruit that year, how well you measure, how the fruit is chopped, and the diameter of your pot. These jams must be checked for setting point. Be sure to leave the test in the freezer long enough for the jam to cool and give an idea of the set. Do not put too much on the plate. Always remove the pot from heat to stop the cooking. Usually the mixture will feel quite viscous when stirred.

Fruitful Trivia _____
When choosing fruit, smell to detect its fruity fragrance. Intense, "peachy" smelling peaches will produce jam that has excellent flavor.

◆ To prevent floating of fruit pieces, such as strawberries, peaches, and pears, stir for five to seven minutes after removing from heat.

◆ Skim foam from the top of jam using a large metal spoon. (Not all jams will have foam.) Some recipes add butter to jam to prevent foaming; I do not like to do this.

Trouble-Shooting Tips and Quick Fixes

In this section, you will find practical tips and information on how to fix or prevent some of the common jam-making errors. A quick read through them may help save problems later. Jams can sometimes become too runny or too stiff. Hopefully yours will turn out just right.

Problem: Jam does not set or is thin and runny.

Some jam will set as soon as it is cooled, while others may take up to 24 hours. If it does not set after this time, check your recipe. If it is an added-pectin jam, check the expiration date on the pectin box. You might want to contact the manufacturer of the pectin, using the toll-free number or website on the box; they may have a solution to try for their particular product.

For jam without added pectin, you may need to cook it a little longer. If the jars have all sealed properly, the contents are safe. Return jam to pot, discard used lids, and begin cooking and testing for setting point. It may take only another couple minutes after it begins to boil to reach setting point. Stir constantly to prevent scorching. Then proceed with sterilized jars and new prepared lids.

Problem: Jam is stiff or tough.

This can occur when fruit is high in natural pectin or if too much pectin is added. Likely the jam was overcooked. To salvage, dilute the jam with fruit juice or a little liqueur, and warm in the microwave to make more spreadable.

Problem: Jam has crystals.

No-cook jam may develop crystals because it was not stirred well enough after the sugar was added. Fruit must be crushed well to extract juice and dissolve the sugar. Cooked jams may crystallize because too much sugar was added (measure accurately using dry measures and scrape top of sugar level with straight edge or knife), or because there was undissolved sugar on the sides of the pan or spoon handle. Stir well during cooking, and scrape down sides with rubber scraper if necessary. Crystallization may result from overcooking or from storing in a place that is too warm or has temperature fluctuations.

Word to the Wise

Read through the entire recipe before beginning, even if you have made it before. Make sure to add ingredients in the order given.

Problem: Floating fruit.

Most fruit will break down during cooking, so this is not always a problem. Fruit will float if it is underripe or undercooked. Ensure that fruit is well crushed or finely chopped. Some fruit are more likely to float than others, especially strawberries, peaches, and pears. To prevent floating, stir mixture for about five minutes after removing from heat. Then pour jam into first jar and wait for about 30 seconds. If fruit pieces float, pour mixture back into the pot and stir a minute or two longer.

Word to the Wise

I define the cook time at the beginning of each recipe as the overall "estimated" cooking time to heat and bring mixtures to a boil as well as the boiling or simmering time specified in the recipe. With preserving (vs. other regular cooking recipes) the time will vary with the type of pot used (metal, glass, size) and how often it is stirred, etc.

Apple Berry Jam

This soft-spreading jam has a not-too-sweet taste and lovely berry flavors. It is ideal to make when you have little bits of fruit left over and there's not enough for any one jam.

Prep time: 25 minutes • Cook time: 25 to 30 minutes • Makes about 6 half-pint jars

2 large apples, peeled, cored, and grated or
finely chopped

2 cups crushed strawberries, about 4 cups
whole strawberries

2 cups raspberries

2 cups red currants or gooseberries

2 TB. lemon juice

5 cups granulated sugar

In a Dutch oven or large heavy-bottomed pot, mix together apples, strawberries, raspberries, and red currants or gooseberries and lemon juice. Bring to boil over high heat, stirring occasionally. Reduce heat; simmer for about seven minutes or until softened, stirring occasionally.

Well Defined

Fingertip tight means to tighten jar ring with just your fingertips gripping it, just until the ring is snug, but not as tight as it will go. Overtightening prevents air from escaping the jar during processing to provide a good seal. Also, tightening rings after processing is likely to disturb and weaken the seal.

Stir in sugar over medium heat until dissolved. Increase heat to high; bring to full boil, stirring constantly. Boil rapidly for 12 to 15 minutes until jam thickens, stirring often. Test for setting point.

Remove from heat; skim off any foam.

Ladle into sterilized jars to within ¼ inch of rim; wipe rims. Apply prepared lids and rings; tighten rings just until *fingertip tight*.

Process jars in boiling water canner for five minutes.

Let rest at room temperature until set. Check seals; refrigerate any unsealed jars for up to three weeks.

Brandied Apricot Jam

The apricot skins intensify the flavor and orange color of this soft-set jam. The liqueur may be omitted.

Prep time: 20 minutes   •   Cook time: 30 to 35 minutes   •   Makes about 5 half-pint jars

8 cups sliced or chopped pitted apricots, about 5 lbs.

4½ cups granulated sugar

3 TB. brandy or apricot brandy (optional)

In a Dutch oven or large heavy-bottomed pot, place apricots.

Stir in sugar over medium heat until dissolved. Increase heat to high; bring to full boil, stirring constantly. Boil rapidly for 20 to 25 minutes or until jam thickens, stirring often. Test for setting point.

Remove from heat; stir in brandy, if using. Skim off any foam.

Ladle into sterilized jars to within ¼ inch of rim; wipe rims. Apply prepared lids and rings; tighten rings just until fingertip tight.

Process jars in boiling water canner for five minutes.

Let rest at room temperature until set. Check seals; refrigerate any unsealed jars for up to three weeks.

Variation

Spiced Apricot Jam: Omit brandy; stir in ¾ tsp. ground cinnamon and ¼ tsp. ground nutmeg after skimming off any foam.

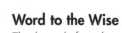

Word to the Wise

The kernels found inside apricot pits were once included in jam recipes, but are no longer considered safe as they contain a toxic compound.

Black Currant Jam

Just black currants—a solo performance with all the berry flavor you enjoy.

Prep time: 10 minutes • Cook time: 35 to 40 minutes • Makes about 7 half-pint jars

6 cups black currants

4 cups water

6 cups granulated sugar

In a Dutch oven or large heavy-bottomed pot, place currants and water; bring to boil over high heat. Reduce heat; simmer for 15 minutes or until softened, stirring occasionally. Use a potato masher to crush currants, if desired.

Stir in sugar over medium heat until dissolved. Increase heat to high; bring to full boil, stirring constantly. Boil rapidly for 6 to 10 minutes until jam thickens, stirring constantly. Test for setting point.

Remove from heat; skim off any foam.

Fruitful Trivia

Black currants are used to make a liqueur called crème de cassis.

Ladle into sterilized jars to within ¼ inch of rim; wipe rims. Apply prepared lids and rings; tighten rings just until fingertip tight.

Process jars in boiling water canner for five minutes.

Let rest at room temperature until set. Check seals; refrigerate any unsealed jars for up to three weeks.

Black Currant Apple Jam

Black currants and apples combine well to produce great flavor and texture. This jam is a good choice when you have a smaller quantity of berries available.

Prep time: 25 minutes   •   Cook time: 30 to 35 minutes   •   Makes about 4 half-pint jars

3 cups black currants

¾ cup water

4 cups coarsely grated peeled apples that soften, 3 to 4 apples or about 1 lb.

4 cups granulated sugar

In a Dutch oven or large heavy-bottomed pot, place currants and water; bring to boil over high heat. Reduce heat; simmer for five minutes or until slightly softened, stirring occasionally. Use a potato masher to crush currants, if desired.

Stir in apples; return to boil over high heat. Reduce heat; boil gently for about 10 minutes or until apples are softened, stirring occasionally.

Stir in sugar over medium heat until dissolved. Increase heat to high; bring to *full boil*, stirring constantly. Boil rapidly for 12 to 14 minutes until jam thickens, stirring often. Test for setting point.

Remove from heat; skim off any foam.

Ladle into sterilized jars to within ¼ inch of rim; wipe rims. Apply prepared lids and rings; tighten rings just until fingertip tight.

Process jars in boiling water canner for five minutes.

Let rest at room temperature until set. Check seals; refrigerate any unsealed jars for up to three weeks.

Well Defined _____

Full boil is a boil that cannot be stirred down and that bubbles constantly and vigorously.

Black and Red Currant Jam

The strong black currant taste is modified here by the red currants, giving you the best of both. The result has a deep red color and sets well, as currants are rich in natural pectin.

Prep time: 15 minutes • Cook time: 30 to 35 minutes • Makes about 5 half-pint jars

4 cups black currants

4 cups red currants

½ cup water

4½ cups granulated sugar

In a Dutch oven or large heavy-bottomed pot, place black and red currants and water; bring to boil over high heat. Reduce heat; cover and simmer for 15 minutes or until softened. Use a potato masher to crush currants, if desired.

Fruitful Trivia
Tiny and tart, fresh currants are not related to dried currants used in baking—dried currants are made from seedless grapes, originally from the area around Corinth, Greece, from which the currant gets its name.

Stir in sugar over medium heat until dissolved. Increase heat to high; bring to full boil, stirring constantly. Boil rapidly for 10 to 12 minutes until jam thickens, stirring often. Test for setting point.

Remove from heat; skim off any foam.

Ladle into sterilized jars to within ¼ inch of rim; wipe rims. Apply prepared lids and rings; tighten rings just until fingertip tight.

Process jars in boiling water canner for five minutes.

Let rest at room temperature until set. Check seals; refrigerate any unsealed jars for up to three weeks.

Black Currant Rhubarb Jam

A lovely combination jam, possibly made from fruit right in your own backyard!

Prep time: 25 minutes   •   Cook time: 30 to 35 minutes   •   Makes about 5 half-pint jars

4 cups black currants

2 cups water

3 cups diced rhubarb, in ½-inch pieces

5 cups granulated sugar

In a Dutch oven or large heavy-bottomed pot, place currants and water; bring to boil over high heat. Reduce heat; simmer for 15 minutes or until softened. Use a potato masher to crush currants, if desired.

Stir in rhubarb and sugar over medium heat until sugar is dissolved. Increase heat to high; bring to full boil, stirring constantly. Boil rapidly for four to seven minutes until jam thickens, stirring constantly. Test for setting point.

Remove from heat; skim off any foam.

Ladle into sterilized jars to within ¼ inch of rim; wipe rims. Apply prepared lids and rings; tighten rings just until fingertip tight.

Process jars in boiling water canner for five minutes.

Let rest at room temperature until set. Check seals; refrigerate any unsealed jars for up to three weeks.

Word to the Wise

Be sure to trim all the leaves from the rhubarb—they contain oxalic acid, which is toxic to humans.

Blackberry Jam

Blackberries have a lot of natural pectin, so this jam will set well without added pectin. It is dark, with a rich berry taste and soft spread. A Marionberry is a blackberry cross and is the most abundantly grown blackberry, grown exclusively in Oregon.

Prep time: 15 minutes • Cook time: 25 to 30 minutes • Makes about 5 half-pint jars

8 cups blackberries

½ cup water

¼ cup lemon juice

4 cups granulated sugar

In a Dutch oven or large heavy-bottomed pot, mix together blackberries, water, and lemon juice; bring to boil over high heat. Reduce heat; simmer for about five minutes, stirring occasionally.

Fruitful Trivia
Blackberry season is pretty short, so when they're available, freeze blackberries in a single layer on a baking sheet, and then transfer to freezer bags or containers.

Stir in sugar over medium heat until dissolved. Increase heat to high; bring to full boil, stirring constantly. Boil rapidly for 12 to 15 minutes until jam thickens, stirring often. Test for setting point.

Remove from heat; skim off any foam.

Ladle into sterilized jars to within ¼ inch of rim; wipe rims. Apply prepared lids and rings; tighten rings just until fingertip tight.

Process jars in boiling water canner for five minutes.

Let rest at room temperature until set. Check seals; refrigerate any unsealed jars for up to three weeks.

Blueberry Banana Jam

This is a combination that is great to spoon over pancakes and waffles, or to serve with bran muffins.

Prep time: 25 minutes   •   Cook time: 15 to 20 minutes   •   Makes about 6 half-pint jars

4 cups wild or cultivated blueberries

1⅔ cups mashed ripe bananas (about 5 medium)

2 TB. lemon juice

1 (1¼ oz.) pkg. powdered fruit pectin

5 cups granulated sugar

In a Dutch oven or large heavy-bottomed pot, mix together blueberries, bananas, and lemon juice.

Stir in pectin; bring to full boil over high heat, stirring constantly.

Stir in sugar; return to full boil, stirring constantly. Boil hard for one minute, stirring constantly.

Remove from heat; skim off any foam.

Ladle into sterilized jars to within ¼ inch of rim; wipe rims. Apply prepared lids and rings; tighten rings just until fingertip tight.

Process jars in boiling water canner for five minutes.

Let rest at room temperature until set. Check seals; refrigerate any unsealed jars for up to three weeks.

Fruitful Trivia
Wild blueberries are native to North America, and grow in Maine and in Eastern Canada. They have a more intense flavor than tame blueberries.

Blueberry Orange Amaretto Jam

The inspiration for this jam comes from a hot drink called "blueberry tea" where amaretto and orange liqueurs are added to hot tea. Use wild blueberries for best flavor. Great for gift-giving.

Prep time: 25 minutes   •   Cook time: 15 to 20 minutes   •   Makes about 6 half-pint jars

3 cups wild or cultivated blueberries

2 TB. finely grated orange rind

4 large oranges, peeled, sectioned (membranes removed), and chopped

¼ cup lemon juice

6 cups granulated sugar

2 (3 oz.) pouches liquid fruit pectin

¼ cup amaretto or orange liqueur

In a Dutch oven or large heavy-bottomed pot, place blueberries; use potato masher to crush about one third of the blueberries to release some of their juice. Stir in orange rind, oranges, and lemon juice.

Stir in sugar; bring to full boil over high heat, stirring constantly. Boil hard for one minute.

Remove from heat; immediately stir in pectin and liqueur. Skim off any foam.

Ladle into sterilized jars to within ¼ inch of rim; wipe rims. Apply prepared lids and rings; tighten rings just until fingertip tight.

Fast Lane
Remove citrus rind *before* juicing fruit as is more difficult to remove the rind once you have juiced it.

Process jars in boiling water canner for five minutes.

Let rest at room temperature until set. Check seals; refrigerate any unsealed jars for up to three weeks.

Variation

Regular Blueberry Jam: Omit orange rind, oranges, and liqueur; increase blueberries to 4 cups.

Boysenberry Jam

Boysenberries are a hybrid berry—a cross between blackberries, raspberries, and loganberries. If you like berry jams, give this one a try. Some local frozen-fruit suppliers sell boysenberries if they are not grown in your area. This jam is also delicious made with loganberries.

Prep time: 15 minutes   •   Cook time: 20 to 30 minutes   •   Makes about 5 half-pint jars

7 cups boysenberries or loganberries

4 cups granulated sugar

In a Dutch oven or large heavy-bottomed pot, place boysenberries; bring to boil over high heat, stirring occasionally. Reduce heat; simmer for about three minutes or until berries begin to release some juice, stirring often.

Stir in sugar over medium heat until dissolved. Increase heat to high; bring to full boil, stirring constantly. Boil rapidly for 8 to 12 minutes or until jam thickens, stirring often. Test for setting point.

Remove from heat; skim off any foam.

Ladle into sterilized jars to within ¼ inch of rim; wipe rims. Apply prepared lids and rings; tighten rings just until fingertip tight.

Process jars in boiling water canner for five minutes.

Let rest at room temperature until set. Check seals; refrigerate any unsealed jars for up to three weeks.

Fruitful Trivia
Wash boysenberries, and all berries, just before using, and be gentle!

Bumbleberry Jam

This interesting mixture of fruits first appeared in a pie with the same name. There are different versions, some including apples, others without rhubarb.

Prep time: 25 minutes • Cook time: 15 to 20 minutes • Makes about 5 half-pint jars

1 cup crushed strawberries

1 cup each raspberries, wild or cultivated blueberries, and blackberries

1 cup diced rhubarb, in ½-inch pieces

5 cups granulated sugar

1 (3 oz.) pouch liquid fruit pectin

In a Dutch oven or large heavy-bottomed pot, mix together strawberries, raspberries, blueberries, blackberries, and rhubarb; bring to boil, stirring constantly. Reduce heat; simmer for about 10 minutes or until rhubarb is softened.

Stir in sugar. Bring to full boil over high heat, stirring constantly; boil hard for one minute.

Fast Lane

For convenience, freeze rhubarb already cut and measured, and freeze strawberries whole to make this jam later in the summer when the other berries are plentiful.

Remove from heat; immediately stir in pectin. Skim off any foam. Stir for five minutes (this will prevent floating fruit).

Ladle into sterilized jars to within ¼ inch of rim; wipe rims. Apply prepared lids and rings; tighten rings just until fingertip tight.

Process jars in boiling water canner for five minutes.

Let rest at room temperature until set. Check seals; refrigerate any unsealed jars for up to three weeks.

Cherry Jam

Sour cherries make delicious jam. The addition of liqueur heightens the flavor. Great for gift-giving.

Prep time: 25 minutes   •   Cook time: 15 to 20 minutes   •   Makes about 5 half-pint jars

4 cups finely chopped pitted sour cherries

1 TB. lemon juice

1 (1¼ oz.) pkg. powdered fruit pectin

4½ cups granulated sugar

2 TB. amaretto or cherry liqueur (optional)

In a Dutch oven or large heavy-bottomed pot, mix together cherries and lemon juice.

Stir in pectin; bring to full boil over high heat, stirring constantly.

Stir in sugar; return to full boil, stirring constantly. Boil hard for one minute, stirring constantly.

Remove from heat; stir in liqueur, if using. Skim off any foam. Stir for five minutes (this will prevent floating fruit).

Ladle into sterilized jars to within ¼ inch of rim; wipe rims. Apply prepared lids and rings; tighten rings just until fingertip tight.

Process jars in boiling water canner for five minutes.

Let rest at room temperature until set. Check seals; refrigerate any unsealed jars for up to three weeks.

Fruitful Trivia
Michigan is the leading producer of sour (tart) cherries in the United States. Montmorency is the main variety.

Cherry Apricot Jam

Cherries pair well with fresh apricots in this fabulous jam. Pit and freeze cherries to have on hand when apricots come in season.

Prep time: 25 minutes • Cook time: 25 to 30 minutes • Makes about 5 half-pint jars

4 cups chopped pitted apricots, about 2 lbs.

4 cups halved pitted sour cherries

¼ cup lemon juice

4 cups granulated sugar

In a Dutch oven or large heavy-bottomed pot, mix together apricots, cherries, and lemon juice; bring to boil over high heat. Reduce heat; cover and simmer for five minutes.

Stir in sugar over medium heat until dissolved. Increase heat to high; bring to full boil, stirring constantly. Boil rapidly for 15 to 20 minutes until jam thickens, stirring often. Test for setting point.

Remove from heat; skim off any foam.

Ladle into sterilized jars to within ¼ inch of rim; wipe rims. Apply prepared lids and rings; tighten rings just until fingertip tight.

Process jars in boiling water canner for five minutes.

Let rest at room temperature until set. Check seals; refrigerate any unsealed jars for up to three weeks.

Fruitful Trivia

Apricots are not peeled when making jam because of the great flavor, and their velvety skins soften when cooked. Choose plump, firm fruit that feel heavy for their size and are uniformly orange with no green tinges. Ripe fruit will yield when lightly pressed; store slightly underripe fruit at room temperature until ripe, and then refrigerate for up to five days.

Cherry Cran-Raspberry Jam

This lovely red jam uses sweet cherries to contrast with the tartness of the cranberries. Place some in the center of your batter when spooning muffin batter into tins.

Prep time: 25 minutes   •   Cook time: 35 to 40 minutes   •   Makes about 6 half-pint jars

3 cups sweet cherries, halved and pitted, about 1⅓ lb.

3 cups cranberries

3 cups raspberries

4½ cups granulated sugar

In a Dutch oven or large heavy-bottomed pot, mix together cherries, cranberries, raspberries, and sugar. Cover; let stand for two hours.

Bring to boil over medium heat, stirring constantly until sugar is dissolved. Increase heat to high; bring to full boil, stirring constantly. Boil rapidly for 25 to 30 minutes until jam thickens, stirring often. Test for setting point.

Remove from heat; skim off any foam.

Ladle into sterilized jars to within ¼ inch of rim; wipe rims. Apply prepared lids and rings; tighten rings just until fingertip tight.

Process jars in boiling water canner for five minutes.

Let rest at room temperature until set. Check seals; refrigerate any unsealed jars for up to three weeks.

Fruitful Trivia

Luscious deep red Bing cherries are the most popular type of sweet cherry.

Cherry Pear Jam

This jam should be named "Cheery Pear." The sour cherry flavor nicely offsets the sweetness of the pears.

Prep time: 25 minutes   •   Cook time: 15 to 20 minutes   •   Makes about 5 half-pint jars

2½ cups finely chopped, peeled, and cored
Bartlett pears (3 to 4 large pears)

2 cups chopped pitted sour cherries

2 TB. lemon juice

1 (1¾ oz.) pkg. powdered fruit pectin

4½ cups granulated sugar

2 TB. cherry liqueur

In a Dutch oven or large heavy-bottomed pot, mix together pears, cherries, and lemon juice; bring to full boil over high heat. Reduce heat; cover and simmer for about two minutes or until pears are tender.

Stir in pectin; bring to full boil over high heat, stirring constantly.

Fruitful Trivia
There are several different cherry liqueurs, including kirsch (a clear brandy flavored with cherry juice and pits), cherry brandy (made from fermented cherries), and Cherry Herring (a cherry liqueur from Denmark).

Stir in sugar; return to full boil, stirring constantly. Boil hard for one minute, stirring constantly.

Remove from heat; stir in liqueur. Skim off any foam. Stir for five minutes (this will prevent floating fruit).

Ladle into sterilized jars to within ¼ inch of rim; wipe rims. Apply prepared lids and rings; tighten rings just until fingertip tight.

Process jars in boiling water canner for five minutes.

Let rest at room temperature until set. Check seals; refrigerate any unsealed jars for up to three weeks.

Cherry Raspberry Jam

This jam features larger pieces of cherry suspended in raspberry jam. Try this as a filling for chocolate cake or jellyroll. See Vanilla Jelly Roll.

Prep time: 20 minutes   •   Cook time: 15 to 20 minutes   •   Makes about 5 half-pint jars

3 cups pitted halved sour cherries

2½ cups raspberries

2 TB. lemon juice

1 (1¼ oz.) pkg. powdered fruit pectin

4 cups granulated sugar

In a Dutch oven or large heavy-bottomed pot, mix together cherries, raspberries, and lemon juice.

Stir in pectin; bring to full boil over high heat, stirring constantly.

Stir in sugar; return to full boil, stirring constantly. Boil hard for one minute, stirring constantly.

Remove from heat; skim off any foam. Stir for five to seven minutes (this will prevent floating fruit).

Ladle into sterilized jars to within ¼ inch of rim; wipe rims. Apply prepared lids and rings; tighten rings just until fingertip tight.

Process jars in *boiling water canner* for five minutes.

Let rest at room temperature until set. Check seals; refrigerate any unsealed jars for up to three weeks.

Well Defined

A **boiling water canner** is a large pot with a rack, deep enough to process jars in boiling water with one- to two-inch coverage.

Cherries Jubilee Jam (Cherry, Red Currant)

This jam is named after the famous dessert that uses cherries, red currant jam, and cherry brandy. Add a little water or orange juice, warm, and brush over a fruit flan, or pour over vanilla ice cream. Also works well with crêpes.

Prep time: 25 minutes • Cook time: 25 to 30 minutes • Makes about 4 half-pint jars

3 cups red currants

3 cups finely chopped pitted sweet cherries

3½ cups granulated sugar

2 TB. cherry brandy (optional)

In a Dutch oven or large heavy-bottomed pot, place red currants. Using a potato masher, crush currants. Stir in cherries; bring to boil over high heat. Reduce heat; cover and *simmer* for five minutes.

Stir in sugar over medium heat until dissolved. Increase heat to high; bring to full boil, stirring constantly. Boil rapidly for 10 to 12 minutes until jam thickens, stirring often. Test for setting point.

Remove from heat; stir in liqueur, if using. Skim off any foam.

 Well Defined

Simmer is a constant, light bubbling over lower heat that slowly cooks the food.

Ladle into sterilized jars to within ¼ inch of rim; wipe rims. Apply prepared lids and rings; tighten rings just until fingertip tight.

Process jars in boiling water canner for five minutes.

Let rest at room temperature until set. Check seals; refrigerate any unsealed jars for up to three weeks.

Five Berry Jam

This is a wonderful five-berry combination with a deep burgundy color, a bit of tartness, and undertones of black currant. Freeze summer berries as they come in season to have on hand. At home I call this jam "Five Star" because the berries are all stars.

Prep time: minutes   •   Cook time: 25 to 30 minutes   •   Makes about 6 half-pint jars

2 cups each: raspberries, blackberries (boysen-berries or loganberries), black currants, red currants, and gooseberries

5 cups granulated sugar

In a Dutch oven or large heavy-bottomed pot, mix together raspberries, blackberries, black and red currants, and gooseberries bring to boil over high heat. Reduce heat; simmer for five minutes, stirring constantly.

Stir in sugar over medium heat until dissolved. Increase heat to high; bring to full boil, stirring constantly. Boil rapidly for five to seven minutes until jam thickens, stirring constantly. Test for setting point.

Remove from heat; skim off any foam.

Ladle into sterilized jars to within ¼ inch of rim; wipe rims. Apply prepared lids and rings; tighten rings just until fingertip tight.

Process jars in boiling water canner for five minutes.

Let rest at room temperature until set. Check seals; refrigerate any unsealed jars for up to three weeks.

Word to the Wise _____
Do not double recipes. It may overcook fruit or prevent thickening/gelling. Also, the pot may boil over, even though it doesn't look that full.

Gooseberry Jam

Get goosed! Gooseberry jam has a unique flavor that is slightly tart. Gooseberries have abundant natural pectin for a good set. Make this jam with green or red gooseberries.

Prep time: 10 minutes   •   Cook time: 25 to 30 minutes   •   Makes about 5 half-pint jars

7 cups gooseberries

½ cup water

4½ cups granulated sugar

In a Dutch oven or large heavy-bottomed pot, place gooseberries and water; bring to boil over high heat. Reduce heat; simmer for five minutes or until berries are softened, stirring occasionally. (Crush any whole berries with back of spoon.)

Stir in sugar over medium heat until dissolved. Increase heat to high; bring to full boil, stirring constantly. Boil rapidly for 10 to 12 minutes until jam thickens, stirring often. Test for setting point.

Fruitful Trivia
Gooseberries may be frozen whole. Remove from stems, trim away blossom ends (beards), and place berries in freezer storage containers or plastic bags.

Remove from heat; skim off any foam.

Ladle into sterilized jars to within ¼ inch of rim; wipe rims. Apply prepared lids and rings; tighten rings just until fingertip tight.

Process jars in boiling water canner for five minutes.

Let rest at room temperature until set. Check seals; refrigerate any unsealed jars for up to three weeks.

Gooseberry Orange Jam

Oranges give a pleasant flavor boost and perk up the color of the gooseberries.

Prep time: 20 minutes   •   Cook time: 25 to 30 minutes   •   Makes about 4 half-pint jars

5 cups gooseberries

1 TB. grated orange rind

2 large oranges, peeled, sectioned (membranes removed), and chopped

4 cups granulated sugar

In a Dutch oven or large heavy-bottomed pot, mix together gooseberries, orange rind, and oranges; bring to boil over high heat, stirring constantly. Reduce heat; simmer for five minutes or until gooseberries are softened. Crush any whole berries with the back of a spoon.

Stir in sugar over medium heat until dissolved. Increase heat to high; bring to full boil, stirring constantly. Boil rapidly for 10 to 12 minutes until jam thickens, stirring often. Test for setting point.

Remove from heat; skim off any foam.

Ladle into sterilized jars to within ¼ inch of rim; wipe rims. Apply prepared lids and rings; tighten rings just until fingertip tight.

Process jars in boiling water canner for five minutes.

Let rest at room temperature until set. Check seals; refrigerate any unsealed jars for up to three weeks.

Word to the Wise

Preserves are sealed when lids curve inward. Test seal by pressing in center—if lid moves, then it has not sealed, so refrigerate immediately. For stored preserves, discard any in which the lids have popped up.

Kiwi Mango Jam

This jam has a beautiful color and exquisite taste. Delicious in cheesecake—stirred into batter and spooned over top the finished cheesecake.

Prep time: 25 minutes • Cook time: 20 to 25 minutes • Makes about 6 half-pint jars

3 cups chopped kiwi, about 6 large kiwis

3 cups chopped mango, 3 to 4 medium mangoes

2 TB. lemon juice

1 (1¾ oz.) pkg. powdered fruit pectin

5 cups granulated sugar

In a Dutch oven or large heavy-bottomed pot, mix together kiwis, mangoes, and lemon juice.

Stir in pectin; bring to full boil over high heat, stirring constantly.

Stir in sugar; return to full boil, stirring constantly. Boil hard for one minute, stirring constantly.

Remove from heat; skim off any foam. Stir for five to seven minutes (this will prevent floating fruit).

Ladle into sterilized jars to within ¼ inch of rim; wipe rims. Apply prepared lids and rings; tighten rings just until fingertip tight.

Process jars in boiling water canner for five minutes.

Let rest at room temperature until set. Check seals; refrigerate any unsealed jars for up to three weeks.

Variation

Plain green or gold Kiwi Jam: Use 6 cups chopped kiwi and omit mangoes.

Fruitful Trivia

Kiwi, or kiwifruit, originated in China. Plants were brought to New Zealand where New Zealanders became famous for producing the green-fleshed variety we now enjoy. In the late 1990s, a gold variety was developed. It derives its name from the national bird, the "kiwi." Kiwifruit is available from California in the summer.

Kiwi Pineapple Orange Jam

This jam has a beautiful light green and orange color and a nice fresh flavor. Jam may also be made with gold kiwis.

Prep time: 25 minutes   •   Cook time: 15 to 20 minutes   •   Makes about 6 half-pint jars

3 cups diced kiwi, about 9 medium kiwis

1 cup (8 oz.) canned crushed pineapple, including juice

3 medium oranges, peeled, sectioned (membranes removed), and chopped

¼ cup lime juice

1 (1¾ oz.) pkg. powdered fruit pectin

5½ cups granulated sugar

In a Dutch oven or large heavy-bottomed pot, mix together kiwis, pineapple, oranges, and lime juice.

Stir in pectin; bring to full boil over high heat, stirring constantly.

Stir in sugar; return to full boil, stirring constantly. Boil hard for one minute, stirring constantly.

Remove from heat; skim off any foam. Stir for five minutes (this will prevent floating fruit).

Ladle into sterilized jars to within ¼ inch of rim; wipe rims. Apply prepared lids and rings; tighten rings just until fingertip tight.

Process jars in boiling water canner for five minutes.

Let rest at room temperature until set. Check seals; refrigerate any unsealed jars for up to three weeks.

Fruitful Trivia

No need to remove the tiny black kiwi seeds—they are edible and add to the look of the jam.

Kiwi Watermelon Jam

I just thought this would make a nice-looking jam—small wedges of green kiwi in a pink jelly. My first attempt I finely chopped the watermelon but it stayed crunchy after cooking. While standing in the shower I got the idea to purée the watermelon instead. It turned out perfectly and tastes great!

Prep time: 25 minutes • Cook time: 15 to 20 minutes • Makes about 5 half-pint jars

2 cups chopped kiwi, about 6 medium kiwis

2 cups puréed watermelon

¼ cup lemon juice

1 (1¾ oz.) pkg. powdered fruit pectin

5½ cups granulated sugar

In a Dutch oven or large heavy-bottomed pot, mix together kiwis, watermelon purée, and lemon juice.

Stir in pectin; bring to full boil over high heat, stirring constantly.

Stir in sugar; return to full boil, stirring constantly. Boil hard for one minute, stirring constantly.

Remove from heat; skim off any foam. Stir for five to seven minutes (this will prevent floating fruit).

Fast Lane _____
To save time, use seedless watermelon! Approximately 3 cups chopped watermelon will give you 2 cups puréed.

Ladle into sterilized jars to within ¼ inch of rim; wipe rims. Apply prepared lids and rings; tighten rings just until fingertip tight.

Process jars in boiling water canner for five minutes.

Let rest at room temperature until set. Check seals; refrigerate any unsealed jars for up to three weeks.

Spiced Peach Jam

This jam, features whole spices that are left in the jam for extra flavor and interest. Cardamom is a sweet spice commonly used in baking and East Indian cuisine; it can be found at specialty food or bulk stores. Use this jam as cake filling or to fill Vanilla Jelly Roll.

Prep time: 30 minutes   •   Cook time: 25 to 30 minutes   •   Makes about 6 half-pint jars

5 cups finely chopped peeled peaches

12 whole cardamom pods

6 (2-inch) cinnamon sticks

6 whole cloves

1 (1¾ oz.) pkg. powdered fruit pectin

5 cups granulated sugar

In a Dutch oven or large heavy-bottomed pot, mix together peaches and cardamom pods, cinnamon sticks, and cloves. Bring to full boil over high heat; boil for three minutes, stirring constantly. Turn off and let stand for 30 minutes, stirring occasionally.

Stir in pectin; bring to full boil over high heat, stirring constantly.

Stir in sugar; return to full boil, stirring constantly. Boil hard for one minute, stirring constantly.

Remove from heat; skim off any foam. Stir for five to seven minutes (this will prevent floating fruit).

Ladle into sterilized jars to within ¼ inch of rim. Make sure there is a piece of cinnamon stick, two cardamom pods, and a clove in each jar. Wipe rims; apply prepared lids and rings. Tighten rings just until fingertip tight.

Process jars in boiling water canner for five minutes.

Let rest at room temperature until set. Check seals; refrigerate any unsealed jars for up to three weeks.

Variation

Plain Peach Jam: Omit spices.

 Fast Lane

How to peel peaches: Bring medium pot of water to boil over high heat. Place peaches two at a time in water; boil for 20 to 30 seconds. Remove peaches with slotted spoon; immediately immerse in bowl of cold water. Repeat with remaining peaches. When peaches are cool enough to handle, slit down side of peel with paring knife; slip off peel. Cut peaches in half and remove pits.

Spiced Peach Cranberry Jam

This refreshing jam has just a hint of spice to accent the fruit flavors. Pick up frozen cranberries to make this jam when peaches are in season. This jam may also be made with unpeeled nectarines in place of peaches.

Prep time: 25 minutes   •   Cook time: 25 to 30 minutes   •   Makes about 5 half-pint jars

4 cups chopped peeled peaches

3 cups cranberries

4½ cups granulated sugar

½ tsp. ground cinnamon

¼ tsp. ground nutmeg

In a Dutch oven or large heavy-bottomed pot, mix together peaches and cranberries.

Stir in sugar, cinnamon, and nutmeg over medium heat until sugar is dissolved. Increase heat to high; bring to full boil, stirring constantly. Boil rapidly for 15 to 18 minutes until jam thickens, stirring often. Test for *setting point*.

Well Defined _____

Setting point is the point at which the preserve is done, at which the sugar, pectin, and acid come together to create a gel and will set.

Remove from heat; skim off any foam.

Ladle into sterilized jars to within ¼ inch of rim; wipe rims. Apply prepared lids and rings; tighten rings just until fingertip tight.

Process jars in boiling water canner for five minutes.

Let rest at room temperature until set. Check seals; refrigerate any unsealed jars for up to three weeks.

Peach Lavender Jam

Lavender adds a sweet aroma, and delicately enhances the flavor of luscious peaches.

Prep time: 30 minutes   •   Cook time: 10 to 15 minutes   •   Makes about 7 half-pint jars

3 TB. dried organic lavender flowers

⅓ cup boiling water

4 cups finely chopped peeled peaches

¼ cup lemon juice

7¼ cups granulated sugar

2 (3 oz.) pouches liquid pectin

To make lavender infusion: Place lavender in small bowl. Pour boiling water over flowers; cover and let steep for 20 minutes. Strain, reserving liquid; discard lavender.

In a Dutch oven or large heavy-bottomed pot, mix together lavender infusion, peaches, and lemon juice.

Stir in sugar; bring to full boil over high heat, stirring constantly. Boil hard for one minute.

Remove from heat; immediately stir in pectin. Skim off any foam. Stir for five minutes (this will prevent floating fruit).

Ladle into sterilized jars to within ¼ inch of rim; wipe rims. Apply prepared lids and rings; tighten rings just until fingertip tight.

Process jars in boiling water canner for five minutes.

Let rest at room temperature until set. Check seals; refrigerate any unsealed jars for up to three weeks.

Variations

Plain Peach Jam: Omit lavender infusion.

Nectarine Jam: Use unpeeled nectarines in place of peaches.

Fruitful Trivia _____

Only use lavender that has been grown without pesticides and herbicides. Lavender will grow in many areas of the United States (check with your local nursery). It thrives in full sun and well-drained soil. Pick flower stems just as flowers begin to open. Let dry, and then store in covered glass container. Dried lavender flowers are available at some specialty kitchen stores or at herb fairs and growers. (See Appendix B for the lavender websites.)

Peach Pear Jam

A touch of peach brings sparkle to pear jam.

Prep time: 35 minutes • Cook time: 10 to 15 minutes • Makes about 8 half-pint jars

3½ cups crushed, peeled, and cored Bartlett
pears (5 to 6 large pears)

½ cup crushed peeled peaches

¼ cup lemon juice

7½ cups granulated sugar

2 (3 oz.) pouches liquid fruit pectin

In a Dutch oven or large heavy-bottomed pot, mix together pears, peaches, and lemon juice; bring to boil over high heat, stirring constantly. Reduce heat; boil gently for one minute to soften fruit.

Well Defined

Jams are filled to within ¼ inch of the rim of the jar (**head-space**). Leaving this exact space is important for creating the vacuum for a good, safe seal. If filled too full, contents may seep through lid while processing and interfere with the seal.

Stir in sugar; bring to full boil over high heat, stirring constantly. Boil hard for one minute.

Remove from heat; immediately stir in pectin. Skim off any foam. Stir for five minutes (this will prevent floating fruit).

Ladle into sterilized jars to within ¼ inch of rim (*headspace*); wipe rims. Apply prepared lids and rings; tighten rings just until fingertip tight.

Process jars in boiling water canner for five minutes.

Let rest at room temperature until set. Check seals; refrigerate any unsealed jars for up to three weeks.

Peach Raspberry Jam

This is a popular fruit combination that makes an exquisite jam. Great stirred into plain yogurt or used with a little orange juice or liqueur stirred into it to top frozen yogurt or ice cream.

Prep time: 25 minutes   •   Cook time: 10 to 15 minutes   •   Makes about 7 half-pint jars

3½ cups chopped peeled peaches

2 cups raspberries

¼ cup lemon juice

7 cups granulated sugar

2 (3 oz.) pouches liquid fruit pectin

In a Dutch oven or large heavy-bottomed pot, mix together peaches, raspberries, and lemon juice.

Stir in sugar; bring to full boil over high heat, stirring constantly. Boil hard for one minute.

Remove from heat; immediately stir in pectin. Skim off any foam. Stir for five minutes (this will prevent floating fruit).

Ladle into sterilized jars to within ¼ inch of rim; wipe rims. Apply prepared lids and rings; tighten rings just until fingertip tight.

Process jars in boiling water canner for five minutes.

Let rest at room temperature until set. Check seals; refrigerate any unsealed jars for up to three weeks.

Word to the Wise

Cooked jams may crystallize because too much sugar was added (measure accurately using dry measures and scrape top of sugar level with straight edge or knife), or because there was undissolved sugar on the sides of the pan or spoon handle. Stir well during cooking and scrape down sides with rubber scraper, if necessary. Crystallization may result from overcooking or from storing in a place that is too warm.

Ginger Pear and Lime Jam

Fresh and crystallized ginger are both used to give this jam its special flavor and bite. Lime rind and juice give it an interesting taste variation.

Prep time: 35 minutes   •   Cook time: 25 to 30 minutes   •   Makes about 4 half-pint jars

4 cups finely chopped, peeled and cored
Bartlett pears (6 to 7 large pears)

½ cup minced crystallized ginger

2 TB. grated fresh ginger

1 TB. grated lime rind

¼ cup lime juice

4 cups granulated sugar

In large Dutch oven or large heavy-bottomed pot, mix together pears, crystallized and fresh ginger, lime rind, and lime juice.

Stir in sugar over medium heat until dissolved. Increase heat to high; bring to full boil, stirring constantly. Boil rapidly for 12 to 14 minutes until jam thickens, stirring often. Test for setting point.

Fruitful Trivia

The ginger plant is grown for its rhizome, or underground stem, which is the rootlike part we use as a versatile spice. Crystallized ginger is candied ginger that has been cooked in a sugar syrup and sprinkled with sugar. Store in glass jar to preserve freshness.

Remove from heat; skim off any foam.

Ladle into sterilized jars to within ¼ inch of rim; wipe rims. Apply prepared lids and rings; tighten rings just until fingertip tight.

Process jars in boiling water canner for five minutes.

Let rest at room temperature until set. Check seals; refrigerate any unsealed jars for up to three weeks.

Variation

Plain Pear Ginger Jam: Omit lime rind and replace lime juice with lemon juice.

Ginger Pear Jam with Crème de Cacao

Here you go, chocolate lovers—ginger, pears, and chocolate liqueur! This jam is one of my favorites and is perfect to fill a chocolate cake, crêpes, or a jellyroll (see Vanilla Jelly Roll). Warm jam up and serve over waffles; adding a dollop of whipped cream as well.

Prep time: 35 minutes   •   Cook time: 10 to 15 minutes   •   Makes about 6 half-pint jars

5 cups finely chopped, peeled, and cored
Bartlett pears (7 to 8 large pears)

⅓ cup minced crystallized ginger

1 TB. finely grated fresh ginger

1 TB. lemon juice

1 (1¼ oz.) pkg. powdered fruit pectin

4 cups granulated sugar

½ cup *white crème de cacao liqueur*

In a Dutch oven or large heavy-bottomed pot, mix together pears, crystallized and fresh ginger, and lemon juice.

Stir in pectin; bring to *full boil* over high heat, stirring constantly.

Stir in sugar; return to full boil over high heat, stirring constantly. Boil hard for one minute, stirring constantly.

Remove from heat; stir in liqueur. Skim off any foam. Stir for five minutes (this will prevent floating fruit).

Ladle into sterilized jars to within ¼ inch of rim; wipe rims. Apply prepared lids and rings; tighten rings just until fingertip tight.

Process jars in boiling water canner for five minutes.

Let rest at room temperature until set. Check seals; refrigerate any unsealed jars for up to three weeks.

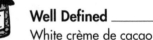

Well Defined

White crème de cacao is a chocolate flavored liqueur that is clear so it adds flavor without changing the color of the jam.

Pears and Port Jam

This jam tastes like pears poached in port. Spoon some over a slice of Brie on a cracker, or use for Baked Brie.

Prep time: 25 minutes • Cook time: 10 to 15 minutes • Makes about 6 half-pint jars

5 cups finely chopped, peeled, and cored
Bartlett pears (7 to 8 large pears)

¾ cup port wine

1 TB. finely grated lemon rind

2 TB. lemon juice

¼ tsp. ground allspice

¼ tsp. ground cinnamon

1 (1¼ oz.) pkg. powdered fruit pectin

4½ cups granulated sugar

In a Dutch oven or large heavy-bottomed pot, mix together pears, port, lemon rind and juice, allspice, and cinnamon.

Stir in pectin; bring to full boil over high heat, stirring constantly.

Fast Lane

Cut up the pears just before making the jam—if left out too long, the flesh will turn brown, which can be prevented with a squeeze of lemon juice or with ascorbic acid powder such as Fruit-Fresh.

Stir in sugar; return to full boil, stirring constantly. Boil hard for one minute, stirring constantly.

Remove from heat; skim off any foam. Stir for five to seven minutes (this will prevent floating fruit).

Ladle into sterilized jars to within ¼ inch of rim; wipe rims. Apply prepared lids and rings; tighten rings just until fingertip tight.

Process jars in boiling water canner for five minutes.

Let rest at room temperature until set. Check seals; refrigerate any unsealed jars for up to three weeks.

Piña Colada Jam (Pineapple, Coconut)

This jam is perfect to warm and serve as a dip for Coconut Shrimp, as a cake filling or for crêpes.

Prep time: 20 minutes   •   Cook time: 15 to 20 minutes   •   Makes about 7 half-pint jars

3½ cups puréed fresh pineapple

1 cup canned *cream of coconut syrup*

⅓ cup white rum

¼ cup lemon juice

6½ cups granulated sugar

2 pouches (3 oz. each) liquid fruit pectin

In a Dutch oven or large heavy-bottomed pot, mix together pineapple purée, cream of coconut syrup, rum, and lemon juice.

Stir in sugar; bring to full boil over high heat, stirring constantly. Boil hard for three minutes, stirring often.

Remove from heat; stir in pectin. Skim off any foam.

Ladle into sterilized jars to within ¼ inch of rim; wipe rims. Apply prepared lids and rings; tighten rings just until fingertip tight.

Process jars in boiling water canner for five minutes.

Let rest at room temperature until set. Check seals; refrigerate any unsealed jars for up to three weeks.

Well Defined

Cream of coconut syrup is available in most supermarkets near the canned milk products or in specialty food stores. Do not confuse with coconut milk, which is not sweet.

Plum Ginger Jam

Ginger is becoming an increasingly popular flavor and is excellent here with plums. Purée this jam to make a delicious plum sauce for dipping chicken fingers.

Prep time: 25 minutes   •   Cook time: 15 to 20 minutes   •   Makes about 4 half-pint jars

5 cups sliced pitted red plums, about 2 lbs. or
15 medium plums

1¾ cups water

1 TB. lemon juice

2 tsp. grated fresh ginger

5 cups granulated sugar

In a Dutch oven or large heavy-bottomed pot, place plums and water; bring to boil over high heat, stirring occasionally. Reduce heat and simmer for about 20 minutes or until softened. Stir in lemon juice and ginger.

Stir in sugar over medium heat until dissolved. Increase heat to high; bring to full boil, stirring constantly. Boil rapidly for 10 to 12 minutes until jam thickens, stirring often. Test for setting point.

Fast Lane

Use a magnetic wand (a plastic wand with a magnet attached to the end) to quickly lift prepared jar lids from hot water. Look for them with the canning tools in kitchen supplies or hardware stores, or check out the Alltrista website listed in Appendix B.

Remove from heat; skim off any foam.

Ladle into sterilized jars to within ¼ inch of rim; wipe rims. Apply prepared lids and rings; tighten rings just until fingertip tight.

Process jars in boiling water canner for five minutes.

Let rest at room temperature until set. Check seals; refrigerate any unsealed jars for up to three weeks.

Variation

Regular Plum Jam: Omit ginger.

Damson Plum Jam

Damson plums are excellent for jams. When they cook, the skin peels back and the flesh softens to release the pit. Look for these plums at farmers' markets in late August to early September.

Prep time: 25 minutes   •   Cook time: 15 to 20 minutes   •   Makes about 6 half-pint jars

7 cups Damson plums, stems removed

2½ cups water

5½ cups granulated sugar

In a Dutch oven or large heavy-bottomed pot, place plums and water; bring to boil over high heat. Reduce heat; boil gently for 15 minutes, stirring occasionally. Use slotted spoon to remove pits.

Stir in sugar over medium heat until dissolved. Increase heat to high; bring to full boil, stirring constantly. Boil rapidly for 8 to 12 minutes until jam thickens, stirring often. Test for setting point.

Remove from heat; skim off any foam.

Ladle into sterilized jars to within ¼ inch of rim; wipe rims. Apply prepared lids and rings; tighten rings just until fingertip tight.

Process jars in boiling water canner for five minutes.

Let rest at room temperature until set. Check seals; refrigerate any unsealed jars for up to three weeks.

 Fast Lane
To speed the process of removing pits, spoon them into strainer over pot; shake to remove extra pulp.

Damson Plum Raspberry Jam

This pairing with raspberries makes a tasty variation on Damson Plum Jam, and is good when you have a small number of plums left over. Try making this recipe with other similar berries such as blackberries, black raspberries, or loganberries in place of raspberries.

Prep time: 25 minutes • Cook time: 15 to 20 minutes • Makes about 6 half-pint jars

7 cups Damson plums, stems removed

1½ cups water

3 cups raspberries

4½ cups granulated sugar

In a Dutch oven or large heavy-bottomed pot, place plums and water; bring to boil over high heat. Reduce heat; simmer for 15 minutes, stirring occasionally. Use slotted spoon to remove pits.

Stir in raspberries and sugar over medium heat until sugar is dissolved. Increase heat to high; bring to full boil, stirring constantly. Boil rapidly for 8 to 12 minutes until jam thickens, stirring often. Test for setting point.

 Fruitful Trivia
Damson plums are small, oval-shape bluish-purple plums that are extremely tart (not a plum for fresh eating) and are ideal for preserves.

Skim off any foam. Ladle into sterilized jars to within ¼ inch of rim. Wipe rims and apply prepared lids and rings; tighten rings just until fingertip tight.

Process jars in boiling water canner for five minutes.

Let rest at room temperature until set. Check seals; refrigerate any unsealed jars for up to three weeks.

Raspberry Jam

This popular jam is a cinch to make. Take advantage of pick-your-own farms to get the best quality and price for raspberries. Freeze whole berries for use later.

Prep time: 25 minutes • Cook time: 15 to 20 minutes • Makes about 6 half-pint jars

9 cups raspberries

4½ cups granulated sugar

3 TB. amaretto liqueur (optional)

In a Dutch oven or large heavy-bottomed pot, place raspberries.

Stir in sugar over medium heat until dissolved. Increase heat to high; bring to full boil, stirring constantly. Boil rapidly for 10 to 12 minutes until jam thickens, stirring often. Test for setting point.

Remove from heat; stir in liqueur, if using. Skim off any foam.

Ladle into sterilized jars to within ¼ inch of rim; wipe rims. Apply prepared lids and rings; tighten rings just until fingertip tight.

Process jars in boiling water canner for five minutes.

Let rest at room temperature until set. Check seals; refrigerate any unsealed jars for up to three weeks.

Word to the Wise

Raspberries are very delicate! Wash just before using by spraying lightly with water and draining well.

Raspberry Blackberry Jam

The addition of blackberries enriches the flavor of the raspberries in this lovely textured jam.

Prep time: 25 minutes • Cook time: 15 to 20 minutes • Makes about 5 half-pint jars

5 cups blackberries

4 cups raspberries

3¾ cups granulated sugar

In a Dutch oven or large heavy-bottomed pot, mix together blackberries and raspberries.

Stir in sugar over medium heat until dissolved. Increase heat to high; bring to full boil, stirring constantly. Boil rapidly for 10 to 15 minutes until jam thickens, stirring often. Test for setting point.

Fruitful Trivia
Blackberries are the largest of the wild berries and are a rich source of natural pectin. They are also cultivated in many areas across the United States and are available from May to August.

Remove from heat, skim off any foam.

Ladle into sterilized jars to within ¼ inch of rim; wipe rims. Apply prepared lids and rings; tighten rings just until fingertip tight.

Process jars in boiling water canner for five minutes.

Let rest at room temperature until set. Check seals; refrigerate any unsealed jars for up to three weeks.

Raspberry Blueberry Jam

I made a delicious pie with these two berries one summer, so I thought I would try them together as a jam. Superb! Great choice to stir into plain yogurt or to top cheesecake.

Prep time: 25 minutes   •   Cook time: 15 to 20 minutes   •   Makes about 4 half-pint jars

3 cups raspberries

2 cups wild or cultivated blueberries

2 TB. lemon juice

3¾ cups granulated sugar

In a Dutch oven or large heavy-bottomed pot, mix together raspberries, blueberries, and lemon juice. Using a potato masher, crush about half the amount of berries to release some of their juice.

Stir in sugar over medium heat until dissolved. Increase heat to high; bring to full boil, stirring constantly. Boil rapidly for 10 to 12 minutes until jam thickens, stirring often. Test for setting point.

Remove from heat; skim off any foam.

Ladle into sterilized jars to within ¼ inch of rim; wipe rims. Apply prepared lids and rings; tighten rings just until fingertip tight.

Process jars in boiling water canner for five minutes.

Let rest at room temperature until set. Check seals; refrigerate any unsealed jars for up to three weeks.

Raspberry Gooseberry Red Currant Jam

These three berries usually arrive mid-summer. This jam has a lovely red color, with a slightly tart taste.

Prep time: 15 minutes • Cook time: 25 to 30 minutes • Makes about 7 half-pint jars

4 cups gooseberries

3 cups red currants

3 cups raspberries

6½ cups granulated sugar

In a Dutch oven or large heavy-bottomed pot, mix together gooseberries and red currants. Bring to boil over high heat, stirring often. Reduce heat; simmer for 10 minutes until softened, stirring occasionally.

Stir in raspberries and sugar over medium heat until sugar is dissolved. Increase heat to high; bring to full boil, stirring constantly. Boil rapidly for six to ten minutes until jam thickens, stirring constantly. Test for setting point.

Fruitful Trivia _____
Gooseberries may be removed from stems, bearded, and frozen whole (see Chapter 2 for information on freezing fruit).

Remove from heat; skim off any foam.

Ladle into sterilized jars to within ¼ inch of rim; wipe rims. Apply prepared lids and rings; tighten rings just until fingertip tight.

Process jars in boiling water canner for five minutes.

Let rest at room temperature until set. Check seals; refrigerate any unsealed jars for up to three weeks.

Raspberry Mango Jam

Fragrant sweet mangoes are a delicious accent to the tartness of raspberries. See Low-Fat Raspberry Mango Frozen Cake.

Prep time: 25 minutes   •   Cook time: 10 to 15 minutes   •   Makes about 5 half-pint jars

2 cups raspberries

2 cups finely chopped mango, about 5 to 6 small or 3 large mangoes

2 TB. lemon juice

5 cups granulated sugar

1 pouch (3 oz.) liquid fruit pectin

In a Dutch oven or large heavy-bottomed pot, mix together raspberries, mango, and lemon juice.

Stir in sugar; bring to full boil over high heat, stirring constantly. Boil hard for one minute.

Remove from heat; immediately stir in pectin. Skim off any foam. Stir for five minutes (this will prevent floating fruit).

Ladle into sterilized jars to within ¼ inch of rim; wipe rims. Apply prepared lids and rings; tighten rings just until fingertip tight.

Process jars in boiling water canner for five minutes.

Let rest at room temperature until set. Check seals; refrigerate any unsealed jars for up to three weeks.

Fruitful Trivia

Choose mangoes that have an unblemished, yellow skin tinged with red. (Some varieties such as Alphonse mangoes have all-yellow skin when ripe and buttery flesh.) Keitt mangoes, grown in the United States, are large and meaty with skin that stays green even when ripe. Ripe mangoes will yield slightly to the gentle pressure of your thumb. Place underripe mangoes in a paper bag at room temperature to hasten ripening; refrigerate once ripe.

Raspberry Plum Jam

Tasty little yellow plums, sometimes with a touch of orange-red blush, combine with ever-popular raspberries in this delightful jam. This recipe may be also be made with red plums.

Prep time: 20 minutes • Cook time: 10 to 15 minutes • Makes about 6 half-pint jars

2 cups finely chopped pitted yellow or red plums, about 1½ lb.

2 cups raspberries

¼ cup lemon juice

5 cups granulated sugar

1 pouch (3 oz.) liquid fruit pectin

In a Dutch oven or large heavy-bottomed pot, mix together plums, raspberries, and lemon juice.

Stir in sugar; bring to full boil over high heat, stirring constantly. Boil hard for one minute.

Remove from heat; immediately stir in pectin. Skim off any foam. Stir for five minutes (this will prevent floating fruit).

Fruitful Trivia

The addition of plums makes a rich-tasting raspberry jam that is less seedy than regular raspberry jam.

Ladle into sterilized jars to within ¼ inch of rim; wipe rims. Apply prepared lids and rings; tighten rings just until fingertip tight.

Process jars in boiling water canner for five minutes.

Let rest at room temperature until set. Check seals; refrigerate any unsealed jars for up to three weeks.

Raspberry Red Currant Jam

This is a beautiful red jam with lots of raspberry flavor and a hint of tartness from the red currants. Stir into your favorite baked cheesecake batter or serve with cream cheese and bagels.

Prep time: 10 minutes • Cook time: 25 to 30 minutes • Makes about 5 half-pint jars

2 cups red currants

5 cups raspberries

5¼ cups granulated sugar

In a Dutch oven or large heavy-bottomed pot, place red currants. Using a potato masher, crush currants. Stir in raspberries; bring to full boil over high heat. Reduce heat; cover and simmer for five minutes.

Stir in sugar over medium heat until dissolved. Increase heat to high; bring to full boil, stirring constantly. Boil rapidly for 12 to 15 minutes until jam thickens, stirring often. Test for setting point.

Remove from heat; skim off any foam.

Ladle into sterilized jars to within ¼ inch of rim; wipe rims. Apply prepared lids and rings; tighten rings just until fingertip tight.

Process jars in boiling water canner for five minutes.

Let rest at room temperature until set. Check seals; refrigerate any unsealed jars for up to three weeks.

Raspberry Rhubarb Jam

Two favorite flavors are natural partners in this delicious jam. Use to make Easy Coffee Cake.

Prep time: 20 minutes • Cook time: 10 to 15 minutes • Makes about 5 half-pint jars

2 cups raspberries

2 cups diced rhubarb, in ½-inch pieces

2 TB. lemon juice

6 cups granulated sugar

1 (3 oz.) pouch liquid fruit pectin

In a Dutch oven or large heavy-bottomed pot, mix together raspberries, rhubarb, and lemon juice. Bring to boil over high heat, stirring constantly. Reduce heat; simmer for three minutes, stirring occasionally.

Stir in sugar; bring to full boil over high heat, stirring constantly. Boil hard for one minute.

Fruitful Trivia
Choose rhubarb that is crisp; to store, wrap tightly in a plastic bag and refrigerate for up to three days.

Remove from heat; immediately stir in pectin. Skim off any foam.

Ladle into sterilized jars to within ¼ inch of rim; wipe rims. Apply prepared lids and rings; tighten rings just until fingertip tight.

Process jars in boiling water canner for five minutes.

Let rest at room temperature until set. Check seals; refrigerate any unsealed jars for up to three weeks.

Red Currant Orange Jam

This is a tasty pairing. If desired, heat jam slightly and press through sieve to remove seeds; use to glaze a fruit flan or tart, or drizzle over cheesecake.

Prep time: 20 minutes • Cook time: 20 to 25 minutes • Makes about 5 half-pint jars

5 cups red currants

2 TB. finely grated orange rind

4 large oranges, peeled, sectioned (membranes removed), and chopped

4½ cups granulated sugar

In a Dutch oven or large heavy-bottomed pot, place currants. Using a potato masher, crush currants. Stir in orange rind and oranges; bring to boil over high heat. Reduce heat; cover and simmer for five minutes.

Stir in sugar over medium heat until dissolved. Increase heat to high; bring to full boil, stirring constantly. Boil rapidly for 7 to 10 minutes until jam thickens, stirring constantly. Test for setting point.

Remove from heat; skim off any foam.

Ladle into sterilized jars to within ¼ inch of rim; wipe rims. Apply prepared lids and rings; tighten rings just until fingertip tight.

Process jars in boiling water canner for five minutes.

Let rest at room temperature until set. Check seals; refrigerate any unsealed jars for up to three weeks.

Fast Lane _____

Remove currants from stems by pulling them upward through the prongs of a fork.

Red Fruit Jam (Red Currant, Raspberry, Cherry)

A blend of three fruits produces wonderful flavor and color in this unique recipe. A little shot of kirsch at the end really gives it a special flavor.

Prep time: 20 minutes • Cook time: 30 to 35 minutes • Makes about 4 half-pint jars

1½ cups chopped pitted sour cherries

1½ cups crushed red currants

1½ cups crushed raspberries

3 cups granulated sugar

1 TB. kirsch or cherry brandy (optional)

In a Dutch oven or large heavy-bottomed pot, mix together cherries, currants, and raspberries; bring to boil over high heat. Reduce heat; simmer for 15 minutes.

Stir in sugar over medium heat until dissolved. Increase heat to high; bring to full boil, stirring constantly. Boil rapidly for 5 to 10 minutes until thickened, stirring often. Test for setting point.

Remove from heat; stir in kirsch, if using. Skim off any foam.

Fruitful Trivia

Kirsch means "cherry" in German. It is also the name of a clear, cherry-based liqueur.

Ladle into sterilized jars to within ¼ inch of rim; wipe rims. Apply prepared lids and rings; tighten rings just until fingertip tight.

Process jars in boiling water canner for five minutes.

Let rest at room temperature until set. Check seals; refrigerate any unsealed jars for up to three weeks.

Rhubarb Orange Ginger Jam

Orange adds lovely color and flavor to rhubarb. A little snap of ginger is added for those who love the taste, but it can be omitted.

Prep time: 25 minutes • Cook time: 25 to 30 minutes • Makes about 4 half-pint jars

4 cups chopped rhubarb, ½-inch pieces

2 TB. grated orange rind

3 medium oranges, peeled, sectioned (membranes removed), and chopped

4½ cups granulated sugar

¼ cup minced crystallized ginger (optional)

In a Dutch oven or large heavy-bottomed pot, mix together rhubarb, orange rind, and oranges. Bring to boil over high heat, stirring constantly. Reduce heat; simmer for five minutes.

Stir in sugar and ginger, if using; stir over medium heat until sugar is dissolved. Increase heat to high; bring to full boil, stirring constantly. Boil rapidly for 10 to 15 minutes until jam thickens, stirring constantly. Test for setting point.

Remove from heat; skim off any foam.

Ladle into sterilized jars to within ¼ inch of rim; wipe rims. Apply prepared lids and rings; tighten rings just until fingertip tight.

Process jars in boiling water canner for five minutes.

Let rest at room temperature until set. Check seals; refrigerate any unsealed jars for up to three weeks.

Fruitful Trivia

When rhubarb is abundant, wash and cut into ½-inch pieces and store in pre-measured quantities in freezer bags or containers. Add directly to jam from frozen state if desired.

Rhubarb Pineapple Jam

The tartness of rhubarb and the sweetness of pineapple complement each other very well in this interesting jam. Use to make Pineapple Tartlets or brush over grilled chicken, pork chops, or roasted ham.

Prep time: 20 minutes • Cook time: 15 to 20 minutes • Makes about 6 half-pint jars

3 cups diced rhubarb, in ½-inch pieces

2 cups (16 oz.) canned crushed pineapple, including juice

1 (1¼ oz.) pkg. powdered fruit pectin

5½ cups granulated sugar

2 TB. apricot brandy or peach schnapps (optional)

In a Dutch oven or large heavy-bottomed pot, mix together rhubarb and pineapple. Cover; simmer for about two minutes or until rhubarb is tender. Stir in pectin.

Bring to full boil over high heat, stirring constantly.

Stir in sugar; return to full boil, stirring constantly. Boil hard for one minute.

Word to the Wise

The timing for pectin-added jams should be exact, so use a timer. Check expiration date on the box of pectin before beginning. Do not interchange liquid and powdered pectin in recipes. Mix in pectin well.

Remove from heat; stir in apricot brandy, if using. Skim off any foam. Stir for five minutes (this will prevent floating fruit).

Ladle into sterilized jars to within ¼ inch of rim; wipe rims. Apply prepared lids and rings; tighten rings just until fingertip tight.

Process jars in boiling water canner for five minutes.

Let rest at room temperature until set. Check seals; refrigerate any unsealed jars for up to three weeks.

Saskatoon Berry (Juneberry) Jam

These dark purple berries have large seeds and grow wild (and are cultivated) in many parts of Canada, especially in the prairies, where they are known as Saskatoons (named after the Canadian city in Saskatchewan). In the United States, they are called juneberries, shadberries, and serviceberries. They have a distinctive taste you don't forget. Warm this jam, dilute with a little water (orange juice or liqueur) and serve over pancakes or waffles.

Prep time: 15 minutes   •   Cook time: 15 to 20 minutes   •   Makes about 6 half-pint jars

6 cups Saskatoon (juneberries)

3 TB. lemon juice

5 cups granulated sugar

1 tsp. ground cinnamon

2 (3 oz.) pouches liquid fruit pectin

In a Dutch oven or large heavy-bottomed pot, mix together saskatoons (juneberries) and lemon juice; crush with a potato masher. Bring to boil over high heat. Reduce heat; cover and simmer for 15 minutes or until berries are softened.

Stir in sugar and cinnamon. Bring to full boil, stirring constantly. Boil hard one minute.

Remove from heat; immediately stir in pectin. Stir for five minutes (this will prevent floating fruit).

Ladle into sterilized jars to within ¼ inch of rim; wipe rims. Apply prepared lids and rings; tighten rings just until fingertip tight.

Process jars in boiling water canner for five minutes.

Let rest at room temperature until set. Check seals; refrigerate any unsealed jars for up to three weeks.

Word to the Wise

It is no longer considered a safe practice to use paraffin on top of preserves. When cooled, paraffin wax tends to contract and may pull away from the sides of the jars. Tiny pinholes can also penetrate through the wax to the surface of the preserve. It is nearly impossible to see the holes with the naked eye. Air and microorganisms can enter the jar and may cause spoilage.

Strawberry Gooseberry Jam

In this jam, gooseberries provide pectin needed for setting. A little orange rind adds an extra touch of flavor.

Prep time: 25 minutes • Cook time: 25 to 30 minutes • Makes about 5 half-pint jars

4 cups gooseberries

4 cups sliced strawberries

4 cups granulated sugar

2 TB. grated orange rind (optional)

In a Dutch oven or large heavy-bottomed pot, mix together gooseberries and strawberries. Bring to boil; simmer for five minutes, stirring occasionally.

Stir in sugar and orange rind over medium heat until sugar is dissolved. Increase heat to high; bring to full boil, stirring constantly. Boil rapidly for 10 to 15 minutes until jam thickens, stirring often. (Crush any whole gooseberries with back of spoon.) Test for setting point.

Fruitful Trivia
Gooseberries have high, natural levels of pectin and are great for pairing with lower pectin fruits. No added pectin is need for a good set.

Remove from heat; skim off any foam.

Ladle into sterilized jars to within ¼ inch of rim; wipe rims. Apply prepared lids and rings; tighten rings just until fingertip tight.

Process jars in boiling water canner for five minutes.

Let rest at room temperature until set. Check seals; refrigerate any unsealed jars for up to three weeks.

Strawberry Kiwi Jam

Strawberries and kiwis have complementary flavors and give this jam a nice texture. Stir it into your favorite cheesecake batter or enjoy with cream cheese and bagels.

Prep time: 25 minutes • Cook time: 10 to 15 minutes • Makes about 5 half-pint jars

2 cups crushed strawberries

2 cups finely chopped kiwi, about 6 medium kiwis

1 (1¾ oz.) pkg. powdered fruit pectin

3½ cups granulated sugar

In a large Dutch oven or large heavy-bottomed pot, mix together strawberries and kiwis.

Stir in pectin; bring to full boil over high heat, stirring constantly.

Stir in sugar; return to full boil, stirring constantly. Boil hard for one minute, stirring constantly.

Remove from heat; skim off any foam. Stir for five minutes (this will prevent floating fruit).

Ladle into sterilized jars to within ¼ inch of rim; wipe rims. Apply prepared lids and rings; tighten rings just until fingertip tight.

Process jars in boiling water canner for five minutes.

Let rest at room temperature until set. Check seals; refrigerate any unsealed jars for up to three weeks.

Fruitful Trivia
The strawberry is related to the rose family, and is native to both of the Americas and Europe. Wild strawberries are worth the picking, if you can find them. They have all the flavor of a large strawberry squeezed into a tiny one!

Strawberry Lavender Jam

Lavender adds a touch of sweetness and aroma to strawberries in this jam. (For information about lavender, see the Fruitful Trivia sidebar in the Peach Lavender Jam recipe earlier in this chapter.)

Prep time: 25 minutes • Cook time: 10 to 15 minutes • Makes about 7 half-pint jars

3 TB. dried organic lavender flowers

⅓ cup boiling water

3½ cups crushed strawberries

¼ cup lemon juice

7 cups granulated sugar

1 (3 oz.) pouch liquid fruit pectin

To make lavender infusion: In small bowl, place lavender. Pour boiling water over flowers; let steep for 20 minutes. Strain; discard lavender.

In a Dutch oven or large heavy-bottomed pot, mix together lavender infusion, strawberries, and lemon juice.

Stir in sugar; bring to full boil over high heat, stirring constantly. Boil hard for one minute.

Fast Lane

To quickly remove the hull from strawberries, poke a large straw from the pointed end up toward the green part. The hull pops right out!

Remove from heat; immediately stir in pectin. Skim off any foam. Stir for five minutes (this will prevent floating fruit).

Ladle into sterilized jars to within ¼ inch of rim; wipe rims. Apply prepared lids and rings; tighten rings just until fingertip tight.

Process jars in boiling water canner for five minutes.

Let rest at room temperature until set. Check seals; refrigerate any unsealed jars for up to three weeks.

Strawberry Margarita Jam

Margaritas ... if you like the drink, you'll love the jam! The flavor is intoxicating. Try it as a topping for cheesecake or mixed with cream cheese on bagels or crackers.

Prep time: 25 minutes   •   Cook time: 10 to 15 minutes   •   Makes about 6 half-pint jars

3 cups crushed strawberries

¾ cup lime juice

⅔ cup tequila

¼ cup orange liqueur

6 cups granulated sugar

1 (3 oz.) pouch liquid fruit pectin

In a Dutch oven or large heavy-bottomed pot, mix together strawberries, lime juice, tequila, and liqueur.

Stir in sugar; bring to full boil over high heat, stirring constantly. Boil hard for one minute.

Remove from heat; immediately stir in pectin. Skim off any foam. Stir for five minutes (this will prevent floating fruit).

Ladle into sterilized jars to within ¼ inch of rim; wipe rims. Apply prepared lids and rings; tighten rings just until fingertip tight.

Process jars in boiling water canner for five minutes.

Let rest at room temperature until set. Check seals; refrigerate any unsealed jars for up to three weeks.

Word to the Wise

Do not use a food processor to crush strawberries or you will get a purée (mush!), and jam will not have a good texture. Crush strawberries one layer at a time in a wide bowl (or glass pie plate) using a potato masher.

Strawberry Pineapple Jam

Pineapple adds an interesting taste and texture to this jam. It's an interesting twist on traditional strawberry jam.

Prep time: 25 minutes • Cook time: 10 to 15 minutes • Makes about 6 half-pint jars

2 cups crushed strawberries

2 cups finely chopped fresh pineapple

7 cups granulated sugar

1 (3 oz.) pouch liquid fruit pectin

In a Dutch oven or large heavy-bottomed pot, mix together strawberries and pineapple.

Stir in sugar; bring to full boil over high heat, stirring constantly. Boil hard for one minute.

Fruitful Trivia

The tasty combination of strawberry and pineapple is best with fresh pineapple but may also be made with drained canned crushed pineapple for convenience.

Remove from heat; immediately stir in pectin. Skim off any foam. Stir for five minutes (this will prevent floating fruit).

Ladle into sterilized jars to within ¼ inch of rim; wipe rims. Apply prepared lids and rings; tighten rings just until fingertip tight.

Process jars in boiling water canner for five minutes.

Let rest at room temperature until set. Check seals; refrigerate any unsealed jars for up to three weeks.

Strawberry Raspberry Jam

Prep time: 20 minutes   •   Cook time: 25 to 30 minutes   •   Makes about 5 half-pint jars

Here are two all-time favorite fruits in one incredible jam!

3½ cups raspberries

3 cups crushed strawberries

⅓ cup lemon juice

4½ cups granulated sugar

In a Dutch oven or large heavy-bottomed pot, mix together raspberries, strawberries, lemon juice, and sugar; let stand for 10 minutes.

Cook over medium heat, stirring constantly until sugar is dissolved. Increase heat to high; bring to full boil, stirring constantly. Boil rapidly for 15 to 18 minutes until jam thickens, stirring often. Test for setting point.

Ladle into sterilized jars to within ¼ inch of rim; wipe rims. Apply prepared lids and rings; tighten rings just until fingertip tight.

Process jars in boiling water canner for five minutes.

Let rest at room temperature until set. Check seals; refrigerate any unsealed jars for up to three weeks.

Fruitful Trivia

Frozen fruit is great for making preserves. Make a family outing to a pick-your-own berry patch and fill your freezer when fruit is in season.

Strawberry Rhubarb Orange Jam

Here I have added orange peel, which provides a lovely variation to this classic jam. It may be left out if you want to make straight Strawberry Rhubarb Jam.

Prep time: 25 minutes • Cook time: 30 to 35 minutes • Makes about 4 half-pint jars

4 cups diced rhubarb, in ½-inch pieces

3 cups chopped strawberries

4 TB. lemon juice

3 TB. finely grated orange rind (optional)

4½ cups granulated sugar

In a Dutch oven or large heavy-bottomed pot, mix together rhubarb, strawberries, lemon juice, and orange rind, if using.

Stir in sugar over medium heat until dissolved. Increase heat to high; bring to full boil, stirring constantly. Boil rapidly for 20 to 25 minutes until jam thickens, stirring often. Test for setting point.

Remove from heat, skim off any foam.

Ladle into sterilized jars to within ¼ inch of rim; wipe rims. Apply prepared lids and rings; tighten rings just until fingertip tight.

Process jars in boiling water canner for five minutes.

Let rest at room temperature until set. Check seals; refrigerate any unsealed jars for up to three weeks.

The Least You Need to Know

◆ Jams can range from simple, one-fruit-and-sugar mixtures to multiple fruit medleys, and mixtures with spices or added liqueurs.

◆ Jams made with commercial pectin require more sugar but give a greater yield for the amount of fruit used. Commercial pectins are natural fruit pectins, extracted from apples or the peel of citrus fruit.

◆ Up to 25 percent underripe fruit can be used when making non-pectin-added jams, as it is higher in pectin than ripe fruit.

◆ To prevent floating of some fruits, stir jam five to seven minutes before ladling into jars.

◆ For jam without added pectin, you may need to cook it a little longer. If the jars have all sealed properly, the contents are safe.

Notes

Notes

Chapter 4

Special Jams and Spreads

In This Chapter

- ◆ No-cook jams, light jams, and no-sugar spreads
- ◆ The role of commercial pectin
- ◆ Tips for expert ease with special jams and spreads
- ◆ What to do to prevent or fix errors

This chapter is going to focus on three special types of jams: no-cook jams, low-sugar jams, and no-sugar spreads. No-cook jams are jams that are made without cooking and have added fruit pectin to aid gelling. They retain a fresh-fruit flavor. Low-sugar jams are jams that have a reduced amount of sugar and have added fruit pectin, specially developed for lower amounts of sugar to aid gelling. No-sugar spreads are not considered to be jams. They are fruit mixtures sweetened with sugar substitutes (low-calorie sweeteners) and have added fruit pectin, specially developed for lower amounts of sugar and sugar substitutes to aid gelling.

Some recipes in this chapter are for no-cook jams made with regular amounts of sugar; some use specially devised pectin for lower sugar; and a couple cooked spreads are made with sugar substitutes. I have included a

Word to the Wise

Always use the exact amount of sugar or sweetener called for in any of these recipes. If you reduce it, the jam or spread may not set or keep.

variety of recipes from Kraft Canada, Inc., and Alltrista Corp. (owner of Bernardin Canada, Ltd., and Ball Corporation in the United States), who make these special products. (These types of jams are not within the area of my expertise but because I have tried them or have demonstrated them at cooking classes and found them to be very good, I wanted to include a few of them for you to try.)

No-Cook Jams

The advantages of no-cook jams, apart from the obvious, are that they do not require sterilized equipment or processing, the fruit is not cooked so it keeps more of its fresh-fruit taste, and it takes a lot less time to make than cooked jams. They also make a great family activity for youngsters who can help with preparation of fruit (for example, crushing berries), measuring of ingredients, stirring, and so on, without the danger of the stove or hot liquids.

No-cook jams used to be called "freezer jams." The name was changed because they do not need to be frozen; they can also be kept, for a limited time, in the refrigerator.

No Cooking Required!

No-cook jams retain their fresh-fruit flavor and are thickened by adding commercial pectin in liquid or powdered form (regular, light, or no-sugar needed). The pectin found naturally in the fruit may be too low or not easily released as it is not heated or cooked. (Cooking concentrates pectin in the fruit via evaporation enough for gelling to occur.) No-cook jams (formerly called freezer jams) may be refrigerated for up to three weeks, or frozen for longer storage. Because jams will be kept at cold temperatures, there's no need to sterilize containers; just wash with soapy water, rinse, and dry with a clean towel. Use jars or good-quality freezer containers. Alltrista Corp. makes plastic lids that fit their canning jars and are perfect for no-cook jams.

Word to the Wise

Just because some jams have less sugar doesn't mean it's okay to eat twice as much, or you may just as well enjoy regular jams. Jams generally do not contain any fat but do contain carbohydrates from both the fruit and the sugar. Any extra calories we consume are converted by the body and stored as fat.

Choose good-quality, ripe fruit, and trim blemishes. Chop or crush fruit according to recipe. Stir in sugar thoroughly, and then let stand to allow sugar to dissolve and juice to come out of the fruit.

Each pectin product has its own recipe leaflet containing numerous recipes, found inside the box. You may contact the companies directly using their websites.

Lighten Up

People with restricted diets may be looking for jams that have less or no sugar.

The texture of light and no-sugar jams may be a little different from regular jams, and they usually have a softer spread. Those made with sugar substitutes will not taste the same as if sugar were used. However, if you must watch your sugar intake carefully, they can be a reasonable alternative. You will find the jams featured here to be very tasty.

Lower-sugar (less-sugar) or no-sugar-needed pectins are special formulations designed to work with less sugar than regular liquid or powdered pectins.

Word to the Wise

Please review Chapter 1 to reacquaint yourself with preserve-making. Things may have changed since you first started making preserves. If you are a beginner, there are a few important things to know before getting started. Many instructions are common to all preserves so, once you get it right for one, you'll sail through the others. It's a lot easier than you might think.

Tips for Prizewinning Special Jams and Spreads

Stop here before beginning to cook for tips on how to get expert results:

◆ Choose top-quality, firm, ripe fruit. Up to 25 percent underripe fruit can be used when making non-pectin-added jams, as it is higher in pectin than ripe fruit. Be meticulous in your preparation of the fruit. Trim any bad spots or blemishes; chop thoroughly and slice evenly.

◆ Measure carefully. When adding the sugar, stir well to ensure that it is completely dissolved, scraping down any that gets on the sides of the bowl (for no-cook jams), pot, or spoon handle. Undissolved sugar can crystallize in your jam. For cooked jams, heating the fruit a little before stirring in the sugar will help the sugar dissolve more quickly.

- Stir and watch your jam; pectin-added jams require a full boil, constantly stirred. Simmered jams with natural pectin will thicken as they cook; reduce temperature and stir more often to prevent scorching.

- The timing for pectin-added jams should be exact; use a timer. Check expiration date on the box of pectin before beginning. Do not interchange liquid pectin and crystals in recipes. Mix in pectin well.

- To prevent floating of fruit pieces, such as strawberries, peaches, and pears, stir for five to seven minutes after removing from heat.

- Skim foam from the top of jam using a large metal spoon. (Not all jams will have foam.) Some recipes add butter to jam to prevent foaming; I do not like to do this.

Troubleshooting Tips and Quick Fixes

In this section, you will find practical tips and information on how to fix or prevent some of the common jam-making errors. A quick read through them may help save problems later. Jams can sometimes become too runny or too stiff. Hopefully yours will turn out just right.

Problem: Jam does not set, or is thin and runny.

Some jam will set as soon as it is cooled, while others may take up to 24 hours. If it does not set after this time, check your recipe. If it is an added-pectin jam, check the expiration date on the pectin box. You might want to contact the manufacturer of the pectin, using the toll-free number or website on the box; they may have a solution to try for their particular product.

Problem: Jam is stiff or tough.

This can occur when fruit is high in natural pectin or if too much pectin is added. Likely the jam was overcooked. To salvage, dilute the jam with fruit juice or a little liqueur and warm in the microwave to make more spreadable.

Word to the Wise

Read through the entire recipe before beginning, even if you have made it before. Make sure to add ingredients in the order given.

Problem: Jam has crystals.

No-cook jam may develop crystals because it was not stirred well enough after the sugar was added. Fruit must be crushed well to extract juice and dissolve the sugar. Cooked jams may crystallize because too much sugar was added (measure accurately using dry measures and scrape top of sugar level with straight edge or knife), or because there was undissolved sugar on the sides of the bowl (for no-cook jams), pan, or spoon handle. Stir well during cooking and scrape down sides with rubber scraper, if necessary. Crystallization may result from over-cooking or from storing in a place that is too warm or has temperature fluctuations.

Problem: Floating fruit.

Most fruit will break down during cooking, so this is not always a problem. Fruit will float if it is underripe or undercooked. Ensure that fruit is well crushed or finely chopped. Some fruit are more likely to float than others, especially strawberries, peaches, and pears. To prevent floating, stir mixture for about five minutes after removing from heat. Then pour jam into first jar and wait for about 30 seconds. If fruit pieces float, then pour mixture back into the pot and stir a minute or two longer.

Word to the Wise

I define the cook time at the beginning of each recipe as the overall "estimated" cooking time to heat and bring mixtures to a boil as well as the boiling or simmering time specified in the recipe. With preserving (vs. other regular cooking recipes) the time will vary with the type of pot used (metal, glass, size) and how often it is stirred, etc.

Peach Blueberry No-Cook Jam

Fragrant fresh peaches and blueberries get a chance to show off in this tasty jam. Stir some into pancake batter or bake into the center of muffins. (Recipe courtesy Kraft Canada, Inc.)

Prep time: 25 minutes • Cook time: No cooking required • Makes about 6 cups

2 cups finely chopped peeled peaches, 4 to 6 medium peaches

1 cup crushed wild or cultivated blueberries

¼ cup lemon juice

5 cups granulated sugar

¾ cup water

1 (1¼ oz.) pkg. Sure Jell powdered fruit pectin

In a large bowl, mix together peaches, blueberries, and lemon juice. Stir in sugar; let stand for 10 minutes.

In a small saucepan, whisk together water and pectin. Bring to boil over high heat; boil for one minute, whisking constantly. Remove from heat.

Stir prepared pectin into fruit mixture; stir for three minutes or until most of sugar is dissolved.

Pour into jars or plastic freezer containers to within ½ inch of rim to allow for expansion; wipe rims. Cover with tight lids; let rest at room temperature until set (may take 24 hours).

Refrigerate for up to three weeks; freeze for longer storage.

Fast Lane

How to peel peaches: Bring a medium pot of water to boil over high heat. Place peaches two at a time in water; boil for 20 to 30 seconds. Remove peaches with slotted spoon; immediately immerse in bowl of cold water. Repeat with remaining peaches. When peaches are cool enough to handle, slit down side of peel with a paring knife; slip off peel. Cut peaches in half and remove pits.

Strawberry Banana No-Cook Jam

A little of this jam in your breakfast shake will get you going in the morning! Stir some into plain yogurt or serve over ice cream. (Recipe courtesy Bernardin Canada, Ltd.)

Prep time: 25 minutes • Cook time: No cooking required • Makes about 5 half-pint jars

1½ cups crushed strawberries, about 1 quart

¾ cup well-mashed ripe banana, 2 to 3 medium bananas

4½ cups granulated sugar

1 (3 oz.) pouch Ball Fruit Jell liquid pectin

½ cup lemon juice

In a large bowl, mix together strawberries and bananas. Stir in sugar; mix well. Let stand for 10 minutes.

Stir in pectin. Add lemon juice; stir for three minutes.

Ladle into jars or plastic freezer containers to within ½ inch of rim to allow for expansion; wipe rims. Cover with tight lids; let rest at room temperature until set (may take 24 hours).

Refrigerate for up to three weeks; freeze for longer storage.

Word to the Wise

Do not use a food processor to crush strawberries or you will get a purée (mush!), and the jam will not have a good texture. Crush strawberries one layer at a time in a wide bowl (or glass pie plate) using a potato masher. Try a fork for mashing bananas.

Strawberry Maple No-Cook Jam

This Kraft recipe has a lovely maple flavor. Serve it slightly warmed and spooned over pancakes and waffles. Try it on crêpes or over ice cream. (Recipe courtesy Kraft Canada, Inc.)

Prep time: 25 minutes • Cook time: No cooking required • Makes about 6 cups

1¾ cups crushed strawberries

1 large orange, peeled, sectioned (membranes removed), and finely chopped

¾ cup maple syrup

¼ cup lemon juice

3¼ cups granulated sugar

¾ cup water

1 (1¾ oz.) pkg. Sure Jell powdered fruit pectin

In a large bowl, mix together strawberries, orange, maple syrup, and lemon juice. Stir in sugar; let stand for 10 minutes.

In a small saucepan, whisk together water and pectin. Bring to boil over high heat; boil for one minute, whisking constantly. Remove from heat.

Stir pectin into prepared fruit mixture; stir for three minutes or until most of sugar is dissolved.

Fruitful Trivia
New York, Vermont, and Quebec, Canada, are the top producers of maple syrup.

Ladle into jars or plastic freezer containers to within ½ inch of rim to allow for expansion; wipe rims. Cover with tight lids; let rest at room temperature until set (may take 24 hours).

Refrigerate for up to three weeks; freeze for longer storage.

Peach Raspberry *Light* No-Cook Jam

Enjoy fresh-fruit flavors in this no-cook jam. Use it to fill an angel-food cake (sliced into three layers) and serve with vanilla frozen yogurt or raspberry or mango ice for a light, low-fat dessert. (Recipe courtesy Kraft Canada, Inc.)

Prep time: 25 minutes　•　Cook time: No cooking required　•　Makes about 5 cups

2 cups finely chopped peeled peaches

1¾ cups crushed raspberries

3¼ cups granulated sugar

1 (1¾ oz.) pkg. Sure Jell Fruit Pectin for
Lower-Sugar Recipes

In a large bowl, mix together peaches and raspberries.

In a separate bowl, mix together ¼ cup sugar and pectin. Gradually add to fruit, stirring well. Let stand for 30 minutes, stirring occasionally.

Stir in remaining sugar; stir for three minutes or until most of sugar is dissolved.

Pour into jars or plastic freezer containers to within ½ inch of rim to allow for expansion; wipe rims. Cover with tight lids; let rest at room temperature until set (may take 24 hours).

Word to the Wise
Be sure to thoroughly stir in sugar.

Refrigerate for up to three weeks; freeze for longer storage.

Raspberry Kiwi *Light* No-Cook Jam

I love to eat these two fruits together fresh, and they make a delicious jam. Serve with vanilla frozen yogurt or raspberry ice, and angel-food or low-fat pound cake. (Recipe courtesy Kraft Canada, Inc.)

Prep time: 20 minutes • Cook time: No cooking required • Makes about 6 cups

3 cups crushed raspberries

1 cup finely chopped kiwi, about 3 peeled kiwis

3¼ cups granulated sugar

1 (1¾ oz.) pkg. Sure Jell Fruit Pectin for Lower-Sugar Recipes

In a large bowl, mix together raspberries and kiwis.

In a separate bowl, mix together ¼ cup sugar and pectin. Gradually add to fruit, stirring well. Let stand for 30 minutes, stirring occasionally.

Fruitful Trivia _____ To freeze raspberries, wash gently, and dry well on paper towels; lay whole berries in single layer on baking sheet; freeze completely; transfer to freezer bags or containers.

Stir in remaining sugar; stir for three minutes or until most of sugar is dissolved.

Pour into jars or plastic freezer containers to within ½ inch of rim to allow for expansion; wipe rims. Cover with tight lids; let rest at room temperature until set (may take 24 hours).

Refrigerate for up to three weeks; freeze for longer storage.

Blackberry Apple Spread

This tasty spread can also be made using 4 cups unsweetened applesauce to save time; skip step 1. (Recipe courtesy Bernardin Canada, Ltd.)

Prep time: 25 minutes   •   Cook time: 15 to 20 minutes   •   Makes about 6 half-pint jars

7 medium apples that soften, about 2½ lbs.

2 cups water

2 cups blackberries, lightly crushed

1 TB. finely grated lemon rind

¼ cup lemon juice

1 (1¾ oz.) pkg. Ball 100 Percent Natural Fruit Jell No-Sugar-Needed pectin

1¾ cups artificial sweetener (type that measures equivalent to sugar)

Slice unpeeled apples into eight wedges each, removing stem and blossom ends. Place in a Dutch oven or large heavy-bottomed pot with 1 cup water; bring to boil over high heat. Reduce heat; cover and simmer for 10 minutes or until apples are softened. Press through a sieve.

Measure exactly 4 cups apple pulp; return to pot (discard apple peels and cores).

Stir in blackberries, lemon rind, and juice and ¾ cup water. Very slowly whisk in pectin. Bring to full boil over high heat, stirring constantly. Boil hard for one minute, stirring constantly.

In a small bowl, dissolve sweetener in remaining ¼ cup water; stir into fruit. Stir for two minutes.

Ladle into sterilized jars to within ¼ inch of rim; wipe rims. Apply prepared lids and rings; tighten rings just until fingertip tight.

Process jars in boiling water canner for five minutes.

Let rest at room temperature until set. Check seals; refrigerate any unsealed jars up to three weeks.

Fruitful Trivia

Making this delicious spread is a great way to use up apples that have lost their crunch!

Tropical Tango Spread (Banana Mango Orange)

Use this exotic-tasting spread with toast or spread on banana bread. (Recipe courtesy Bernardin Canada, Ltd.)

Prep time: 25 minutes • Cook time: 15 to 20 minutes • Makes about 4 half-pint jars

2 cups puréed mango (3 or 4 mangoes)

1 cup mashed ripe banana, 2 or 3 bananas
(not puréed)

2 cups orange juice

2 TB. lemon juice

1 (1¼ oz.) pkg. Ball 100 Percent Natural Fruit
Jell No-Sugar-Needed Pectin

1 cup artificial sweetener (type that measures
equivalent to sugar)

1 tsp. each vanilla and rum extracts

In a Dutch oven or large heavy-bottomed pot, mix together mango, banana, 1¾ cups orange juice, and lemon juice.

Very slowly stir in pectin. Bring to full boil over high heat, stirring constantly. Boil hard for one minute, stirring constantly. Remove from heat.

Word to the Wise

Preserves are sealed when lids curve inward. Test seal by pressing in center—if lid moves, it has not sealed, so refrigerate immediately. For stored preserves, discard anywhere the lids have popped up.

In a small bowl, dissolve sweetener in remaining ¼ cup orange juice; stir into fruit with vanilla and rum extracts. Stir for two minutes.

Ladle into sterilized jars to within ¼ inch of rim; wipe rims. Apply prepared lids and rings; tighten rings just until fingertip tight.

Process jars in boiling water canner for five minutes.

Let rest at room temperature until set. Check seals; refrigerate any unsealed jars up to three weeks.

The Least You Need to Know

♦ No-cook jams are fresh tasting and easy to make because heat is not used which can destroy flavor. Fruit retains its fresh-picked flavor and the method is simplified from cooked jams.

♦ No-cook jams do not need to be processed because they are always refrigerated or frozen. Cold prevents microorganisms from multiplying too quickly, freezing stops microbial growth.

♦ Special pectins have been developed to set no-cook and no-sugar spreads. They are a different formulation from regular liquid pectin.

Notes

Notes

_____

_____

_____

_____

_____

_____

_____

_____

_____

_____

_____

_____

_____

_____

_____

_____

_____

_____

_____

_____

_____

_____

_____

Chapter 5

Conserves

In This Chapter

- What is a conserve?
- Tips for expert ease with conserves
- How to test for doneness
- What to do to prevent or fix errors

Conserves are fruit mixtures usually made with two or more fruits, sugar, dried fruit, nuts, and sometimes spices or liquor; they are cooked and are slightly thinner in consistency than jam but should mound up on spoon.

At one time, conserves were eaten alone as a dessert. We now typically eat them as we do jams, on our favorite bread, toast, scone, or muffin. They can also be used to top cake or ice cream, or stirred into fresh yogurt.

Conserves have a soft jamlike consistency but are different from jams. They usually contain dried fruit, such as raisins, apricots, cranberries, and cherries, and often include chopped or whole nuts. The combination of dried fruit and nuts gives these preserves a bit of a chewy and crunchy texture when eaten. Alcohol, in the form of rum or fruit liqueur, enhances the flavor and makes it a little more special for gift giving. (Note that if you prefer, nuts and liquor can be omitted from any of the recipes.)

Let Your Creative Juices Flow

The pieces of fruit used in conserves are somewhat larger than pieces used for jams; for example, fruit is halved or sliced instead of chopped. Conserves can be uniquely stylized to suit individual preferences by varying the type of dried fruit, using whole or toasted nuts, changing the nuts, or varying the liqueur. Because of their uniqueness, conserves are not something you can easily buy.

Conserves are usually cooked down to thicken, so they do not normally require added pectin, nor do they need to be made with high-pectin fruit. Firm, slightly underripe fruit is used because it is higher in natural pectin than riper fruit; overripe fruit is lower in pectin and loses its shape more easily when cooked.

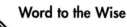

Word to the Wise

Please review Chapter 1 to reacquaint yourself with preserve-making. Things may have changed since you first started making preserves. If you are a beginner, there are a few important things to know before you get started. Many instructions are common to all preserves so, once you get it right for one, you'll sail through the others. It's a lot easier than you might think.

Tips for Prizewinning Conserves

Stop here before beginning to cook for tips on how to get expert results:

- Use slightly underripe or firm just-ripe fruit; avoid soft overripe fruit. Wash well. Pare away any blemishes or bruises.

- Measure carefully. When adding sugar, stir well to ensure that it is completely dissolved, scraping down any that gets on the sides of the pot or spoon handle. Undissolved sugar can crystallize in your conserve. Heating the mixture a little before stirring in the sugar will help the sugar dissolve more quickly.

- If desired, soak dried fruit in water overnight; drain before adding. Dried fruit is usually added about halfway through the cooking time to retain its texture; nuts are added near the end as they need no cooking. Liqueurs are also added at the end to retain flavor.

- Stir and watch your conserve. Dried fruit may sink to the bottom and scorch if insufficiently stirred. Conserves are not cooked as long as jams without added pectin, so watch them and test for doneness (see the following section) to avoid overcooking.

- After removing from heat, let rest one minute, and then stir to evenly distribute dried fruit and nuts in your mixture.

Test for Doneness

Place a spoonful of conserve on a chilled plate; place in freezer for a minute or two until cooled to room temperature. Gently push the mixture with your finger and it will slightly wrinkle when done. When cooled, it will have the texture of a soft jam. You want it to be able to mound on a spoon when serving but be soft enough to tumble from it. If it becomes sticky, it has been overcooked. To remedy, stir in a little apple juice, orange juice, or water; reheat, stirring constantly.

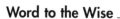 **Word to the Wise** ___

Read through the entire recipe before beginning, even if you have made it before. Make sure to add ingredients in the order given.

Word to the Wise _____

I define the cook time at the beginning of each recipe as the overall "estimated" cooking time to heat and bring mixtures to a boil as well as the boiling or simmering time specified in the recipe. With preserving (vs. other regular cooking recipes) the time will vary with the type of pot used (metal, glass, size) and how often it is stirred, etc.

Troubleshooting Tips and Quick Fixes

In this section, you will find practical tips and information on how to fix or prevent some of the common conserve-making errors. A quick read through them may help save problems later. Jams can sometimes become too runny or too stiff. Hopefully yours will turn out just right.

Problem: Conserve is thin and runny.

It's likely conserve needs to be cooked longer—if the jars have all sealed properly, the contents are safe. Return conserve to pot, discard used lids, and begin cooking and testing again. It might take only another few minutes after it begins to boil; stir constantly. Then proceed with sterilized jars and new prepared lids.

Problem: Conserve is too stiff or tough.

It's likely conserve was overcooked—if it has not yet been put into jars, you can try to thin it by adding a little fruit juice or water; return to boil and test for doneness.

Problem: Conserve has crystals.

Too much sugar may have been added (measure accurately using dry measures and scrape top of sugar level with straight edge or knife), or undissolved sugar may have coated the sides of the pan or spoon handle. Stir well during cooking and scrape down sides with rubber scraper, if necessary. Crystallization may result from over-cooking or from storing in a place that is too warm or has temperature fluctuations.

Problem: Dried fruit or nuts settled to bottom of jar.

Wait a minute or two after removing conserve from heat; stir to evenly distribute fruit and/or nuts throughout mixture.

Apple Orange Apricot Conserve

Make this tasty conserve with apples, oranges, and dried fruit any time of year. Great to use in or on muffins.

Prep time: 35 minutes • Cook time: 55 to 65 minutes • Makes about 6 half-pint jars

3 large oranges

3 large apples that keep their shape, peeled, cored, and chopped, in ½-inch pieces

2 cups water

4½ cups granulated sugar

½ tsp. ground cinnamon

¾ cup diced dried apricots

¾ cup golden seedless raisins

⅓ cup coarsely chopped pecans or walnuts (optional)

¼ cup apricot or orange liqueur (optional)

Slice unpeeled oranges into round slices about ⅛-inch thick; cut each round into 12 to 14 wedges. In a Dutch oven or large heavy-bottomed pot, mix together oranges, apples, and water; bring to boil over high heat, stirring often. Reduce heat; cover and boil gently for 30 minutes or until orange peels are softened.

Stir in sugar and cinnamon; bring to boil over high heat, stirring constantly.

Reduce heat; boil gently, uncovered, for 15 minutes, stirring often. Stir in apricots and raisins; cook 10 to 15 minutes longer until mixture reaches soft jamlike consistency, stirring often. Test for doneness. Stir in pecans and liqueur, if using; cook for about two minutes longer, stirring constantly.

Remove from heat; let rest for one minute. Stir to distribute dried fruit and nuts.

Ladle into sterilized jars to within ¼ inch of rim; wipe rims. Apply prepared lids and rings; tighten rings just until fingertip tight.

Process jars in boiling water canner for five minutes.

Let rest at room temperature until set. Check seals; refrigerate any unsealed jars for up to three weeks.

Word to the Wise

Stir conserves frequently to prevent scorching.

Apricot Almond Conserve

Fresh apricots, with their deep orange and red peels, give a wonderful flavor to this lightly spiced conserve. For a deeper color and flavor, substitute packed brown sugar for the granulated sugar.

Prep time: 25 minutes • Cook time: 40 to 45 minutes • Makes about 6 half-pint jars

3 lbs. ripe apricots, pitted and sliced or chopped

4 cups granulated sugar

1 cup golden seedless raisins

1½ tsp. ground cardamom

½ tsp. ground allspice

½ tsp. ground cinnamon

⅓ cup blanched whole almonds (optional)

⅓ cup *amaretto* liqueur, or ½ tsp. almond extract (optional)

In a Dutch oven or large heavy-bottomed pot, mix together apricots, sugar, raisins, cardamom, allspice, and cinnamon. Bring to boil over high heat, stirring constantly.

Reduce heat; boil gently for 30 to 35 minutes, stirring often. Cook until mixture reaches soft jamlike consistency, stirring often. Test for doneness. Stir in almonds and liqueur or extract, if using; cook for about two minutes longer, stirring constantly.

Remove from heat; let rest for one minute. Stir to distribute dried fruit and nuts.

Well Defined

Amaretto is an almond-flavored liqueur that is often made from the kernels of apricot pits.

Ladle into sterilized jars to within ¼ inch of rim; wipe rims. Apply prepared lids and rings; tighten rings just until fingertip tight.

Process jars in boiling water canner for five minutes.

Let rest at room temperature until set. Check seals; refrigerate any unsealed jars for up to three weeks.

Cherry Raspberry Apple Conserve

This deep-red conserve has a nice cherry-almond flavor. Serve with English muffins.

Prep time: 30 minutes • Cook time: 35 to 40 minutes • Makes about 5 half-pint jars

3 cups pitted, halved sour cherries

2 cups raspberries

2 large apples that keep their shape, peeled, cored, and chopped, in ½-inch pieces

4½ cups granulated sugar

1 TB. grated lemon rind

1 TB. lemon juice

⅓ cup slivered blanched almonds (optional)

¼ cup amaretto or cherry liqueur (optional)

In a Dutch oven or large heavy-bottomed pot, mix together cherries, raspberries, apples, sugar, lemon rind, and lemon juice.

Bring to boil over high heat, stirring constantly. Reduce heat; boil gently for 25 to 30 minutes until mixture reaches a soft jamlike consistency, stirring often. Reduce heat further and stir more often as mixture thickens. Test for doneness. Stir in nuts and amaretto, if using; simmer for two minutes longer.

Remove from heat; let rest for one minute. Stir to distribute nuts.

Ladle into sterilized jars to within ¼ inch of rim; wipe rims. Apply prepared lids and rings; tighten rings just until fingertip tight.

Process jars in boiling water canner for five minutes.

Let rest at room temperature until cooled. Check seals; refrigerate any unsealed jars for up to three weeks.

Fruitful Trivia

Sour cherries are also called tart cherries. Look for cherries that are medium-firm with a glossy surface. Store in plastic bag in the refrigerator. Look for cherry pitters in gourmet kitchen shops.

Fig and Italian Plum Conserve

This conserve is a wonderful mixture of Mediterranean flavors. It has a beautiful deep-red color and rich flavor. Toasted pine nuts give it a unique touch. Delicious served over soft goat cheese on crackers or sliced baguette. If desired, sprinkle freshly toasted pine nuts over top of conserve when serving this appetizer.

Prep time: 30 minutes • Cook time: 60 to 70 minutes • Makes about 5 half-pint jars

2 lbs. Italian purple plums, pitted, coarsely
chopped or sliced

1 lb. ripe fresh figs, coarsely chopped or sliced

2½ cups granulated sugar

½ cup liquid honey

½ cup sweet sherry

2 tsp. finely grated lemon rind

¼ cup lemon juice

1 (6-inch) cinnamon stick, broken into
3 pieces

⅓ cup toasted pine nuts (optional)

In a Dutch oven or large heavy-bottomed pot, mix together plums, figs, sugar, honey, sherry, lemon rinds, lemon juice, and cinnamon stick. Bring to boil over high heat, stirring constantly.

Fruitful Trivia ____ Buy fresh figs that are slightly soft and sweet smelling, with undamaged skin. They have a soft flesh with many tiny, edible seeds. They can be stored in refrigerator for several days, but use soon after purchase. Calimyrna are a variety of fig grown in California that have green skins and white flesh.

Reduce heat; boil gently for 50 to 60 minutes, stirring often. Cook until mixture reaches soft jamlike consistency, stirring often. Test for doneness. Stir in pine nuts, if using; cook for about two minutes longer, stirring constantly.

Remove from heat; let rest for one minute. Stir to distribute nuts.

Ladle into sterilized jars to within ¼ inch of rim; wipe rims. Apply prepared lids and rings; tighten rings just until fingertip tight.

Process jars in boiling water canner for five minutes.

Let rest at room temperature until set. Check seals; refrigerate any unsealed jars for up to three weeks.

Nectarine Apricot Cherry Conserve

This conserve was developed for my friend Wendi, who loves nectarines. Dried cherries, which can be found at bulk stores, add a bit of tartness.

Prep time: 40 minutes   •   Cook time: 50 to 60 minutes   •   Makes about 6 half-pint jars

8 cups chopped pitted nectarines (do not peel)

1 TB. finely grated lemon rind

¼ cup lemon juice

4½ cups granulated sugar

1 cup sliced dried apricots

1 cup dried cherries or cranberries

2 TB. apricot brandy (optional)

In a Dutch oven or large heavy-bottomed pot, mix together nectarines, lemon rind, and lemon juice. Bring to boil over high heat, stirring constantly. Reduce heat; cover and simmer for 12 to 15 minutes or until softened.

Stir in sugar, apricots, and cherries; return to boil, stirring constantly. Reduce heat; boil gently for 25 to 30 minutes or until mixture reaches soft jamlike consistency, stirring often. Reduce heat further and stir more often as mixture thickens. Test for doneness. Stir in brandy, if using; simmer for one minute longer.

Ladle into sterilized jars to within ¼ inch of rim; wipe rims. Apply prepared lids and rings; tighten rings just until fingertip tight.

Process jars in boiling water canner for five minutes.

Let rest at room temperature until set. Check seals; refrigerate any unsealed jars for up to three weeks.

Fruitful Trivia

Choose nectarines that have a smooth skin with red and yellow coloring. Nectarines should give slightly to the touch. Slightly underripe fruit can be placed in a paper bag and left at room temperature for a couple days to ripen. Avoid fruit that is overly hard or green.

Pear Maple Walnut Conserve

Here, maple-walnut flavor is combined with pears for a sensational taste. Stir some into plain yogurt and top with granola for a great snack, or dot over apples in a pie or apple crisp.

Prep time: 35 minutes   •   Cook time: 15 to 20 minutes   •   Makes about 5 half-pint jars

4½ cups chopped, peeled, and cored pears,
5 to 6 large Bartlett pears

1 TB. lemon juice

1 (1¼ oz.) pkg. powdered fruit pectin

3½ cups granulated sugar

¾ cup maple syrup

¼ cup chopped walnuts (optional)

In a Dutch oven or large heavy-bottomed pot, mix together pears and lemon juice; stir in pectin. Bring to full boil over high heat, stirring constantly.

Word to the Wise

Processing is necessary in order to kill any microorganisms that might have gotten into your preserve while filling the jars. It also gives a higher pressure seal. During processing air is forced out of the jar creating a vacuum. Lids are pulled in as the jar and contents cool.

Stir in sugar; return to full boil, stirring constantly. Boil hard for one minute, stirring constantly.

Remove from heat; stir in maple syrup and nuts, if using. Skim off any foam. Stir for seven minutes (this will prevent floating fruit).

Ladle into sterilized jars to within ¼ inch of rim; wipe rims. Apply prepared lids and rings; tighten rings just until fingertip tight.

Process jars in boiling water canner for five minutes.

Let rest at room temperature until set. Check seals; refrigerate any unsealed jars for up to three weeks.

Caribbean Treasure Conserve (Pineapple, Papaya, Mango)

This conserve brings you the taste of the tropics. Thin with a little orange juice and serve over ice cream, or use to make Fried Bananas Caribbean, Caribbean Chicken, or Fruit Loaf.

Prep time: 40 minutes • Cook time: 45 to 50 minutes • Makes about 6 half-pint jars

2 cups canned crushed pineapple, including juice

2 cups puréed papaya, peeled, with seeds removed

1½ cups diced mango (about 1 large mango)

2 TB. finely grated orange rind

2 medium oranges, peeled, sectioned (membranes removed), and chopped

¼ cup lime or lemon juice

½ tsp. ground allspice

½ tsp. ground cinnamon

4½ cups granulated sugar

⅓ cup amber or coconut rum, or 1 tsp. coconut or rum extract (optional)

⅓ cup toasted slivered almonds (optional)

In a Dutch oven or large heavy-bottomed pot, mix together pineapple, papaya, mango, orange rind, oranges, lime juice, allspice, and cinnamon. Bring to boil over high heat, stirring constantly. Reduce heat; boil gently for five minutes, stirring often.

Stir in sugar; return to boil, stirring constantly. Reduce heat; boil gently for 30 to 40 minutes, stirring often. Cook until mixture reaches soft jamlike consistency, stirring often. Test for doneness. Stir in rum or extract and almonds, if using; cook for two minutes longer, stirring constantly.

Remove from heat; let rest for one minute. Stir to distribute nuts.

Ladle into sterilized jars to within ¼ inch of rim; wipe rims. Apply prepared lids and rings; tighten rings just until fingertip tight.

Process jars in boiling water canner for five minutes.

Let rest at room temperature until set. Check seals; refrigerate any unsealed jars for up to three weeks.

Fruitful Trivia

Look for papayas (sometimes also called pawpaws) that have bright yellow skin and a sweet aroma. Shiny black seeds are edible and have a peppery bite.

Plum Cranberry Orange Conserve

This conserve has a lovely plum and orange flavor, with dried cranberries and whole almonds dispersed throughout. For a different taste, lightly toast the almonds to enhance their flavor. Recipe may also be made with red plums.

Prep time: 30 minutes • Cook time: 35 to 45 minutes • Makes about 4 half-pint jars

4 cups sliced or quartered, pitted small
yellow plums, about 1½ lbs.

Finely grated rind and juice from 3 large
oranges

3½ cups granulated sugar

¾ cup dried cranberries

¼ cup blanched whole almonds (optional)

2 TB. amaretto or orange liqueur (optional)

In a Dutch oven or large heavy-bottomed pot, mix together plums, orange rind and juice, sugar, and dried cranberries. Bring to boil over high heat, stirring constantly.

Reduce heat; boil gently for 20 to 30 minutes, stirring often. Cook until mixture reaches soft jamlike consistency, stirring often. Test for doneness. Stir in almonds and liqueur, if using; cook for two minutes longer, stirring constantly.

Ladle into sterilized jars to within ¼ inch of rim; wipe rims. Apply prepared lids and rings; tighten rings just until fingertip tight.

Process jars in boiling water canner for five minutes.

Let rest at room temperature until set. Check seals; refrigerate any unsealed jars for up to three weeks.

Word to the Wise _____

Stir and watch your conserve. Dried fruit may sink to the bottom and scorch if insufficiently stirred. Conserves are not cooked for as long as jams without added pectin, so watch them and test for doneness (see the "Test for Doneness" section earlier in the chapter) to avoid overcooking.

Christmas Plum Conserve

This delicious, deep-colored conserve, made with Italian plums, is perfectly suited to a festive holiday table.

Prep time: 40 minutes • Cook time: 70 to 80 minutes • Makes about 6 half-pint jars

2 lbs. Italian purple plums

¼ cup water

3¼ cups granulated sugar

1½ cups Thompson raisins

Grated rind and juice from 1 orange and ½ lemon

½ cup chopped walnuts or pecans (optional)

Cut plums in half, discarding stems and pits. In a Dutch oven or large heavy-bottomed pot, mix together plums and water. Bring to boil over high heat, stirring often.

Stir in sugar, raisins, and all the rind and juice; return to boil, stirring constantly. Reduce heat; boil gently for about 45 minutes, stirring often.

Stir in nuts, if using; simmer for 10 to 15 minutes longer or until mixture reaches soft jamlike consistency, stirring often. Reduce heat further and stir more often as mixture thickens. Test for doneness.

Ladle into sterilized jars to within ¼ inch of rim; wipe rims. Apply prepared lids and rings; tighten rings just until fingertip tight.

Process jars in boiling water canner for five minutes.

Let rest at room temperature until set. Check seals; refrigerate any unsealed jars for up to three weeks.

Fruitful Trivia _____
Thompson raisins are the most popular raisins in North America. California is the largest producer.

Strawberry, Rhubarb, and Pear Conserve

In this conserve, pear is added to the classic strawberry-rhubarb combination. Use it to make Easy Coffee Cake.

Prep time: 40 minutes • Cook time: 40 to 50 minutes • Makes about 6 half-pint jars

4 cups diced rhubarb, in ½-inch pieces

3 cups chopped or sliced strawberries

3 cups chopped, peeled, and cored Bartlett pears

⅓ cup lemon juice

6 cups granulated sugar

In a Dutch oven or large heavy-bottomed pot, mix together all ingredients. Bring to boil over high heat, stirring constantly.

Fruitful Trivia
Bartlett pears are the most common of hundreds of varieties of pears grown in North America. Peel just before using (get your other ingredients ready first) as they brown very quickly. Use an ascorbic acid product such as Fruit-Fresh or lemon juice to keep them from browning.

Reduce heat; boil gently for 30 to 40 minutes until mixture reaches a soft jamlike consistency, stirring often. Reduce heat further and stir more often as mixture thickens. Test for doneness.

Ladle into sterilized jars to within ¼ inch of rim; wipe rims. Apply prepared lids and rings; tighten rings just until fingertip tight.

Process jars in boiling water canner for five minutes.

Let rest at room temperature until cooled. Check seals; refrigerate any unsealed jars for up to three weeks.

The Least You Need to Know

◆ Conserves are different from jams, being more upscale with added liqueur, dried fruit, and nuts.

◆ Conserves are great for gift-giving because they are unique and not easy to buy.

◆ Learn how to get the consistency of your conserve just right.

◆ Be careful not to scorch conserves as they thicken; stir and watch carefully.

Notes

Notes

Chapter 6

Mincemeats

In This Chapter

- ◆ What is mincemeat?
- ◆ How to test for doneness
- ◆ How to use mincemeat
- ◆ Tips for expert ease with mincemeat
- ◆ What to do to prevent or fix errors

The recipes in this chapter are for meatless mincemeats. I have included a couple of recipes for fruit mixtures that are not really jams or conserves, but are minced fruit mixtures with dried fruit and nuts; they are ideal for making tarts. Use your favorite pastry recipe, fill unbaked tart shells with mincemeat, and bake. If desired, cut a small top from the pastry with a scalloped-edge or small star cutter, place over filling, and sprinkle with granulated sugar before baking. Or cut a larger round to completely cover the filling, fold over, and pinch to bottom pastry to enclose; cut small slits in top; sprinkle with granulated sugar or brush with egg yolk beaten with 1 teaspoon milk for glossy finish. Bake on cookie sheet.

For an interesting pie, stir 2 cups of either of the following mince-meats into 3 cups chopped apples. Follow directions for double crust pie, cutting steam vents in the top pastry. Bake in a 425°F oven (on the lower rack) for 15 minutes; reduce heat to 350°F and bake for 30 minutes longer or until apples are tender and pastry is golden brown.

> **Word to the Wise** _____
>
> Please review Chapter 1 to reacquaint yourself with preserve-making. Things may have changed since you first started making preserves. If you are a beginner, there are a few important things to know before you get started. Many instructions are common to all preserves so, once you get it right for one, you'll sail through the others. It's a lot easier than you might think.

Tips for Prizewinning Mincemeats

Stop here before beginning to cook for tips on how to get expert results:

◆ Use slightly underripe or firm just-ripe fruit; avoid soft overripe fruit. Wash well. Pare away any blemishes or bruises.

◆ Measure carefully. When adding sugar, stir well to ensure that it is completely dissolved, scraping down any that gets on the sides of the pot or spoon handle. Undissolved sugar can crystallize in your conserve. Heating the mixture a little before stirring in the sugar will help the sugar to dissolve more quickly.

◆ If desired, soak dried fruit in water overnight; drain before adding. Dried fruit is usually added about halfway through the cooking time to retain its texture; nuts are added near the end as they need no cooking. Liqueurs are also added at the end to retain flavor.

> **Fruitful Trivia** _____
>
> Old-fashioned mincemeats are popular in English Christmas pies and tarts and usually include minced beef or beef suet (a type of fat) in the fruit and spice mixture. They would be left to age for a month or so.

◆ Stir and watch your mincemeat. Dried fruit may sink to the bottom and scorch if insufficiently stirred. Test for doneness (see the following section) to avoid overcooking.

◆ After removing from heat, let rest one minute, and then stir to evenly distribute dried fruit and nuts in your mixture.

Test for Doneness

Place a spoonful of mincemeat on a chilled plate; place in freezer for a minute or two until cooled to room temperature. Gently push the mixture with your finger and it will slightly wrinkle when done. When cooled, it will have the texture of a soft jam.

You want it to be able to mound on a spoon when serving but still be soft enough to tumble from it. If it becomes sticky, it has been overcooked. To remedy, stir in a little apple juice, orange juice or water; reheat, stirring constantly.

Troubleshooting Tips and Quick Fixes

In this section, you will find practical tips and information on how to fix or prevent some of the common mincemeat-making errors. A quick read through them may help save problems later. Mincemeats can sometimes become too runny or too stiff. Hopefully yours will turn out just right.

Word to the Wise

Read through the entire recipe before beginning, even if you have made it before. Make sure to add ingredients in the order given.

Problem: Mincemeat is thin and runny.

It's likely mincemeat needs to be cooked longer—if the jars have all sealed properly, the contents are safe. Return mincemeat to pot, discard used lids, and begin cooking and testing again. It might take only another few minutes after it begins to boil; stir constantly. Then proceed with sterilized jars and new prepared lids.

Problem: Mincemeat is too stiff or tough.

It's likely mincemeat was overcooked—if it has not yet been put into jars, you can try to thin it by adding a little fruit juice or water; return to boil and test for doneness.

Problem: Dried fruit or nuts settled to bottom of jar.

Wait a minute or two after removing mincemeat from heat; stir to evenly distribute fruit and/or nuts throughout mixture.

Word to the Wise

I define the cook time at the beginning of each recipe as the overall "estimated" cooking time to heat and bring mixtures to a boil as well as the boiling or simmering time specified in the recipe. With preserving (vs. other regular cooking recipes) the time will vary with the type of pot used (metal, glass, size) and how often it is stirred, etc.

Carrot Apple Mincemeat

This tasty minced fruit mixture is perfect for tarts, or can be used to make Marmalade Pecan Cookies, omitting the pecans from the cookies, or in place of Piña Colada Jam to make Pineapple Tartlets.

Prep time: 35 minutes • Cook time: 60 to 70 minutes • Makes about 5 half-pint jars

4 cups apples that keep their shape, peeled, cored, and chopped

3½ cups packed brown sugar

2½ cups water

2 cups finely grated carrots

1 TB. finely grated lemon rind

2 TB. lemon juice

1 tsp. ground cinnamon

½ tsp. ground nutmeg

1 cup golden seedless raisins

½ cup chopped pecans

In a Dutch oven or large heavy-bottomed pot, mix together apples, brown sugar, water, carrots, lemon rind, lemon juice, cinnamon, and nutmeg. Bring to boil over high heat, stirring constantly. Reduce heat; boil gently for 30 minutes.

Stir in raisins; cook for 20 minutes longer or until mixture reaches soft jamlike consistency, stirring often. Reduce heat further and stir more often as mixture thickens. Test for doneness. Stir in pecans; cook for two minutes longer, stirring constantly.

Fast Lane
Use your food processor to grate carrots. For added convenience, measure 2 cups grated carrot and place in plastic freezer bag (squeezing out extra air) or container and freeze.

Ladle into sterilized jars to within ¼ inch of rim; remove air pockets and wipe rims. Apply prepared lids and rings; tighten rings just until fingertip tight.

Process jars in boiling water canner for 10 minutes.

Let rest at room temperature until cooled. Check seals; refrigerate any unsealed jars for up to three weeks.

Pear and Apple Mincemeat

This flavor-packed, all-fruit mixture (no animal products) can be spooned directly into tart shells and baked. Use in place of Piña Colada Jam to make Pineapple Tartlets.

Prep time: 45 minutes • Cook time: 55 to 60 minutes • Makes about 5 half-pint jars

4 cups diced, peeled, and cored Bartlett pears
(6 to 7 large pears)

2 large apples, peeled, cored, and diced

1 TB. finely grated orange rind

⅓ cup orange juice

1 TB. finely grated lemon rind

¼ cup lemon juice

1½ cups packed brown sugar

¾ cup raisins

½ cup dried currants

¼ cup minced candied ginger

¾ tsp. ground allspice

¾ tsp. ground cinnamon

Pinch salt

⅓ cup chopped pecans (optional)

¼ cup dark rum or 1 tsp. rum extract
(optional)

In a Dutch oven or large heavy-bottomed pot, mix together pears, apples, orange rind, orange juice, lemon rind, lemon juice, brown sugar, raisins, currants, ginger, allspice, cinnamon, and salt. Bring to boil over high heat, stirring constantly.

Reduce heat; boil gently for about 45 minutes or until mixture reaches soft jamlike consistency, stirring often. Reduce heat further and stir more often as mixture thickens. Test for doneness. Stir in pecans and rum, if using. Simmer for two minutes longer, stirring constantly.

Fast Lane

Always remember to grate the lemon or lime rind before cutting and squeezing the fruit for juice! It is much easier to get the rind off if you do it before juicing. Remember to scrub peel well with soapy water to remove surface residue; rinse well.

Ladle into prepared jars to within ½ inch of rim; remove air pockets and wipe rims. Apply prepared lids and rings; tighten rings just until fingertip tight.

Process jars in boiling water canner for 10 minutes.

Let rest at room temperature until cooled. Check seals; refrigerate any unsealed jars for up to three weeks.

The Least You Need to Know

◆ Mincemeat need not contain meat or meat fat and can be made with just fruit.

◆ Minced fruit mixtures make convenient tart fillings or additions to apple pie.

◆ Mincemeat mixtures follow the same guidelines as conserves, in that they are cooked slowly until they thicken. However, they have a longer processing time.

Notes

Notes

Chapter 7

Jellies

In This Chapter

- ◆ What is a jelly?
- ◆ Tips for expert ease with jellies
- ◆ How to use and jelly bag
- ◆ How to get clear gels
- ◆ What to do to prevent or fix errors

Jellies are sparkling clear gels made with strained fruit juice (or other liquids, such as wine) and sugar, and they are cooked, with or without added pectin; they hold their shape but are tender enough to quiver, and they spread easily.

They are different from jams in that they are clear and made with only liquids, such as fruit juice, wine, vinegar, or water, or with liquid infused with herbs. Berries that have large seeds are often made into jellies (for example, elderberries) as well as small fruit with inedible seeds (such as crabapples or Concord grapes). Some people prefer the texture of jellies over jams, or like to use jellies as clear glazes for fruit flans or meats.

A Word About Pectin

Jellies made from fruit with high natural pectin or a combination of high and low pectin will gel without added commercial pectin. When the dripped juice is very thick (viscous), it means it will be rich in pectin. Keeping water to a minimum while the fruit is cooking will give flavorful, thick juice.

Many jellies require the addition of commercial fruit pectin, either liquid or powdered, because they lack enough naturally. Indeed, wine jellies would not be possible without it, nor would some of the other savory jellies infused with herbs or garlic.

Testing, One, Two ...

Jellies were tested for sugar content using a refractometer, so no more sugar was added than was needed for a good set. A refractometer has a delicate prism inside of it. A little of the preserve is placed on its small glass surface. It is held up to the light, and when you look through the eye piece (which looks like a six-inch telescope) the percentage of sugar present shows up on a scale.

Acidity was also tested with a pH meter to ensure sufficient acid for gelling.

Word to the Wise

Please review Chapter 1 to reacquaint yourself with preserve-making. Things may have changed since you first started making preserves. If you are a beginner, there are a few important things to know before getting started. Many instructions are common to all preserves so, once you get it right for one, you'll sail through the others. It's a lot easier than you might think.

How to Use a Jelly Bag

Here is the information you need to know for how to use and care for your jelly bag. Jelly bags are used to extract just the juice from cooked fruit. The juice is then used to make jelly. The pulp, including seeds and fruit peel, are then discarded.

+ Place jelly bag in its holder.
+ Rinse bag by pouring about 2 cups boiling water over it; let drain into sink or container (such as a pot or bowl). This will help to keep the fruit juice from soaking into bag when it is poured through.
+ Set jelly bag over large bowl or pot; pour in cooked fruit and juice.
+ Cover and allow juice to drip slowly through jelly bag overnight.

◆ Discard contents of bag, and then wash the bag with warm, soapy water and allow to dry; store in plastic bag to keep clean. (*Note:* Several layers of cheese-cloth layered in a mesh strainer may be used if you do not have a jelly bag.)

Tips for Prizewinning Jellies

Stop here before beginning to cook for tips on how to get expert results:

◆ Choose just-ripe fruit; about 25 percent can be slightly underripe (underripe fruit is higher in pectin). Cook fruit just until tender; do not overcook or pectin will be destroyed.

◆ Do not squeeze the jelly bag or jelly will be cloudy.

◆ Use only the exact amount of juice specified in the recipe; using extra may result in a jelly that does not set. Juice may be frozen for making jelly later.

◆ Measure sugar accurately and stir well to ensure that it is completely dissolved, scraping down any that gets on the sides of the pot or spoon handle. Heating the juice or liquid a little before stirring in the sugar will help the sugar dissolve more quickly.

Fast Lane

Most of juice will have dripped through after about 4 hours (if you don't want to wait overnight); longer dripping will yield about ½ cup more liquid.

Word to the Wise

To get crystal-clear jellies, do not squeeze the jelly bag. Squeezing the bag causes some of the pulp to come through and will make your jelly cloudy.

◆ Jellies require a full boil to evaporate the liquid and to concentrate the sugar and pectin. Make sure your pot is deep enough; it should be at least four times as deep as the liquid, measured from the inside of the pot. Do not double recipes or add more liquid than called for. The liquid will likely bubble right to the top of the pot. I recommend using the deepest pot you have or, if you make jellies often, investing in a deeper one—six-inch or deeper, with at least a nine-inch inside diameter. Sticky jelly makes a real mess and can cause burns!

◆ The timing for pectin-added jellies should be exact; use a timer. Check expiration date on the box of pectin before beginning.

◆ Jellies without added pectin must be checked for setting point. Jelly will thicken in a sheet once cooled. Always remove the pot from the heat to stop cooking.

- Skim foam from the top of jelly using a large metal spoon (not all jellies will have foam). I do not like to add butter to my jellies, to prevent foaming. To remove small bits of foam that sink or are hard to get, pour through a fine-mesh strainer.

- Work quickly with jellies, as they may set quickly. A tip is to pour them from the pot into a sterilized 4 cup glass measure and then pour mixture quickly into jars. If it begins to set, you may get small bubbles in your jelly.

- Do not seal jellies with paraffin wax. This practice is no longer considered safe. When cooled, paraffin wax tends to contract and pull away from the sides of the jars. Tiny pinholes can also penetrate through the wax to the surface of the preserve. It is nearly impossible to see the holes with the naked eye. Air and micro-organisms can enter the jar and may cause spoilage.

- Do not invert jars after sealing. Process for good seal.

Troubleshooting Tips and Quick Fixes

In this section, you will find practical tips and information on how to fix or prevent some of the common jelly-making errors. A quick read through them may help save problems later. Learn how to prevent trapped bubbles and crystal formation in your jelly. Jellies can be too soft and runny or too stiff and rubbery. Hopefully yours will turn out just right.

Problem: Jelly does not set or is soft.

Some jellies set as soon as they are cooled, while others may take up to 24 hours or longer. If it is an added-pectin recipe, check the expiration date on the pectin box. You might want to contact the manufacturer of the pectin, using the toll-free number or website on the box; they may have a solution to try for their particular product.

For jellies without added pectin, you might need to cook a little longer. If the jars have all sealed properly, then the contents are safe. Return the jelly to the pot, discard used lids, and begin to boil again and test for setting point. It might only take another couple of minutes for it to reach setting point. Then proceed with sterilized jars and new prepared lids.

Jelly may have been overcooked or cooked too slowly for too long. The fruit may have been naturally low in pectin or overripe. In this case, you may only be able to use the jelly as a syrup to pour over pancakes or ice cream or to sweeten fruit salads or compotes.

Problem: Jelly is stiff or tough.

This can occur when fruit is high in natural pectin or when too much pectin is added. Likely it was overcooked; this happens when there is not enough sugar and the mixture takes too long to reach setting point. To salvage, dilute with fruit juice or a little liqueur and warm in the microwave; stir well. It can then be used to pour over pancakes or ice cream, or to sweeten fruit salads or compotes.

Problem: Jelly weeps.

This occurs when liquid seeps from the jelly. Weeping is caused by too much acid in the juice, not enough pectin, or storage of jelly in a place that is too warm or has temperature fluctuations.

Problem: Jelly has small bubbles.

Some jellies begin to set very quickly. If they do, you may get small air bubbles trapped in your jelly. Work quickly, keeping everything hot, and pour mixture quickly into jars.

Problem: Jelly has crystals.

This can occur when too much sugar has been added (may have been measured inaccurately) or when there is undissolved sugar on the sides of the pan or spoon handle. Stir well during cooking and scrape down sides with rubber scraper, if necessary. Crystallization may result from overcooking or from storing jelly in a place that is too warm or has temperature fluctuations.

Word to the Wise
Read through the entire recipe before beginning, even if you have made it before. Make sure to add ingredients in the order given.

Problem: Jelly is cloudy.

Thoroughly wash fruit before cooking. Do not overcook fruit; cook just until tender. If you squeeze the jelly bag, the jelly will become cloudy when cooked.

Word to the Wise
Prep time does not include dripping time. It includes the preparation time for washing and cutting the fruit and for measuring the water and sugar.

I define the cook time at the beginning of each recipe as the overall "estimated" cooking time to heat and bring mixtures to a boil as well as the boiling or simmering time specified in the recipe. With preserving (vs. other regular cooking recipes) the time will vary with the type of pot used (metal, glass, size) and how often it is stirred, etc.

Crabapple Jelly

This tart fruit makes delicious jelly that is deep red. Use this jelly to glaze meats or fruit flans, or with fresh baked scones or muffins.

Prep time: 35 minutes • Cook time: 40 to 50 minutes • Makes about 6 half-pint jars

14 cups crabapples

6 cups water

4½ cups sugar

Cut crabapples in half, and remove stem and blossom ends. In a Dutch oven or large heavy-bottomed pot, place crabapples and water; bring to boil over high heat. Reduce heat to medium and cook for 20 minutes or until very soft. Use a potato masher to further break down apples after about 15 minutes.

Pour through prepared jelly bag; allow to drip without squeezing.

Measure exactly 6 cups liquid (add water if not enough liquid); pour into the Dutch oven.

Stir in sugar over medium heat until dissolved. Increase heat to high; bring to full boil, stirring constantly. Boil for 8 to 12 minutes without stirring until setting point is reached.

Remove from heat; skim off any foam.

Ladle quickly into sterilized jars to within ¼ inch of rim; wipe rims. Apply prepared lids and rings; tighten just until fingertip tight.

Process jars in boiling water canner for five minutes.

Let rest at room temperature until set. Check seals; refrigerate any unsealed jars for up to three weeks.

Word to the Wise

It is no longer considered a safe practice to use paraffin on top of preserves. When cooled, paraffin wax tends to contract and pull away from the sides of the jars. Tiny pinholes can also penetrate through the wax to the surface of the preserve. It is nearly impossible to see the holes with the naked eye. Air and microorganisms can enter the jar and may cause spoilage.

Cran-Raspberry Jelly

This flavor combination, popular as a juice drink, is made here from fresh or frozen fruit.

Prep time: 10 minutes • Cook time: 35 to 40 minutes • Makes about 6 half-pint jars

8 cups raspberries

6 cups cranberries

6 cups water

5¾ cups granulated sugar

In a Dutch oven or large heavy-bottomed pot, mix together raspberries, cranberries, and water. Cover; simmer for 15 minutes or until very soft. Use a potato masher to further break down fruit after about 10 minutes.

Pour through prepared jelly bag; allow to drip without squeezing.

Measure exactly 6 cups liquid (add water if not enough liquid); pour into the Dutch oven.

Stir in sugar over medium heat until dissolved. Increase heat to high; bring to full boil, stirring constantly. Boil for five to eight minutes without stirring, until *setting point* is reached.

Ladle quickly into sterilized jars to within ¼ inch of rim; wipe rims. Apply prepared lids and rings; tighten just until fingertip tight.

Well Defined

The **setting point** is the point at which the preserve is done, at which the sugar, pectin, and acid come together to create a gel and will set.

Process jars in boiling water canner for five minutes.

Let rest at room temperature until set. Check seals; refrigerate any unsealed jars for up to three weeks.

Elderberry Jelly

Elderberries are dark, almost black, berries with large seeds and a taste a bit like both blackberries and blueberries. They grow all over North America and you will likely find them growing wild and need to pick them yourself. Use a fork to strip them from their stalks because this berry can stain your fingers.

Prep time: 20 minutes • Cook time: 25 to 30 minutes • Makes about 6 half-pint jars

5 cups elderberries (removed from stems)

3 cups water

1 (1¼ oz.) pkg. powdered fruit pectin

¼ cup lemon juice

6½ cups granulated sugar

In a Dutch oven or large heavy-bottomed pot, mix together elderberries and water. Bring to full boil over high heat; reduce heat and simmer for 15 minutes or until softened. Mash with a potato masher.

Pour through prepared jelly bag; allow to drip without squeezing.

Measure exactly 4 cups liquid (add water if not enough liquid); pour into the Dutch oven. Stir in pectin and lemon juice. Bring to full boil over high heat, stirring constantly.

Stir in sugar. Return to full boil; boil for one minute, stirring constantly.

Remove from heat; skim off any foam.

Word to the Wise

Jellies are filled to within ¼ inch of the rim of the jar. This "headspace" is required to create the vacuum for a good, safe seal.

Ladle quickly into sterilized jars to within ¼ inch of rim; wipe rims. Apply prepared lids and rings; tighten just until fingertip tight.

Process jars in boiling water canner for five minutes.

Let rest at room temperature until set. Check seals; refrigerate any unsealed jars for up to three weeks.

Concord Grape Jelly

This is the grape jelly of the peanut butter and jelly sandwiches of your childhood. Look for these deep-bluish-purple grapes at farmers' markets in September.

Prep time: 30 minutes   •   Cook time: 40 to 45 minutes   •   Makes about 4 half-pint jars

14 cups stemmed Concord grapes, about 5½ lbs.

1 tart apple, stem and blossom ends removed, sliced

2 cups water

3¾ cups granulated sugar

In a Dutch oven or large heavy-bottomed pot, mix together grapes, apple, and water. Bring to full boil over high heat; boil for 10 minutes or until very soft. Use a potato masher to further break down fruit after about eight minutes.

Pour through prepared jelly bag; allow to drip without squeezing.

Refrigerate for 24 hours to allow granules formed by tartaric acid to settle to bottom. Measure exactly 5 cups of juice, being careful not to include any of the crystals. Pour into the Dutch oven.

Stir in sugar over medium heat until dissolved. Increase heat to high; bring to full boil, stirring constantly. Boil for 15 to 20 minutes, without stirring, until setting point is reached.

Remove from heat; skim off any foam.

Ladle quickly into sterilized jars to within ¼ inch of rim; wipe rims. Apply prepared lids and rings; tighten just until fingertip tight.

Process jars in boiling water canner for five minutes.

Let rest at room temperature until set. Check seals; refrigerate any unsealed jars for up to three weeks.

Fruitful Trivia

Tartaric acid crystals can cause jelly to crystallize after it sets. Do not skip the step of letting it stand for 24 hours.

Peach Vanilla Jelly

A hint of vanilla adds a wonderful flavor accent to this sparkling, orange-colored jelly. The more red on the fruit, the deeper the color will be. This is an easy method for dealing with a lot of peaches in a short time, as you do not peel them. Use to glaze French Apple Tarts.

Prep time: 30 minutes • Cook time: 35 to 40 minutes • Makes about 7 half-pint jars

5 lbs. peaches (not peeled), pitted and sliced, about 10 cups sliced peaches

1½ cups water

1 vanilla bean, split lengthwise

1 (1¾ oz.) pkg. powdered fruit pectin

5¾ cups granulated sugar

In a Dutch oven or large heavy-bottomed pot, mix together peaches, water, and vanilla bean. Bring to boil over high heat; reduce heat and simmer for 20 minutes or until peaches are very soft. Use a potato masher to further break down peaches after about 15 minutes.

Pour through prepared jelly bag; allow to drip without squeezing.

Measure exactly 4 cups liquid; pour into the Dutch oven. Stir in pectin; bring to full boil over high heat, stirring constantly.

Word to the Wise

Vanilla beans may be found in specialty grocery stores, packaged in a glass tube. Do not buy vanilla beans in cardboard packaging, as they are likely dried out.

Stir in sugar. Return to full boil, stirring constantly; boil hard for one minute, stirring constantly.

Remove from heat; skim off any foam.

Ladle quickly into sterilized jars to within ¼ inch of rim; wipe rims. Apply prepared lids and rings; tighten just until fingertip tight.

Process jars in boiling water canner for five minutes.

Let rest at room temperature until set. Check seals; refrigerate any unsealed jars for up to three weeks.

Red Currant Jelly

Red currants make bright-red jelly with a lovely flavor. This recipe is great to make when you have an abundant supply of the fruit; freeze fruit or juice for jelly-making at a later date. Thin the jelly by adding a little water, orange juice, or liqueur and spoon over cheesecake, use it to glaze fruit flan or French Apple Tarts, or serve with Baked Brie.

Prep time: 15 minutes • Cook time: 30 to 35 minutes • Makes about 7 half-pint jars

12 cups red currants, about 3½ lbs.

6 cups water

6 cups granulated sugar

In a Dutch oven or large heavy-bottomed pot, mix together currants and water; bring to full boil over high heat. Reduce heat; simmer for 10 to 15 minutes or until very soft. Use a potato masher to further break down currants after about 10 minutes.

Pour through prepared jelly bag; allow to drip without squeezing.

Measure exactly 6 cups liquid (add water if not enough liquid); pour into the Dutch oven.

Stir in sugar over medium heat until dissolved. Increase heat to high; bring to full boil, stirring constantly. Boil for five to eight minutes without stirring, until setting point is reached.

Remove from heat; skim off any foam.

Ladle quickly into sterilized jars to within ¼ inch of rim; wipe rims. Apply prepared lids and rings; tighten just until fingertip tight.

Process jars in boiling water canner for five minutes.

Let rest at room temperature until set. Check seals; refrigerate any unsealed jars for up to three weeks.

 **Fast Lane**
Remove currants from stems by pulling them upward through the prongs of a fork.

Red Currant Raspberry Jelly

The red currants in this jelly are set off by a bit of raspberry flavor. It makes a terrific glaze for fruit flans or topping for cheesecake.

Prep time: 15 minutes • Cook time: 30 to 35 minutes • Makes about 3½ half-pint or 7 (4 oz.) jelly jars

7 cups red currants, about 2 lbs.

5 cups raspberries

2 cups water

3¾ cups granulated sugar

In a Dutch oven or large heavy-bottomed pot, mix together currants, raspberries, and water; bring to full boil over high heat. Reduce heat; simmer for 10 to 15 minutes or until very soft. Use a potato masher to further break down fruit after about 10 minutes.

Pour through prepared jelly bag; allow to drip without squeezing.

Measure exactly 4 cups liquid (add water if not enough liquid); pour into the Dutch oven.

Stir in sugar over medium heat until dissolved. Increase heat to high; bring to full boil, stirring constantly. Boil for eight to ten minutes without stirring until setting point is reached.

Remove from heat; skim off any foam.

Ladle quickly into sterilized jars to within ¼ inch of rim; wipe rims. Apply prepared lids and rings; tighten just until fingertip tight.

Process jars in boiling water canner for five minutes.

Let rest at room temperature until set. Check seals; refrigerate any unsealed jars for up to three weeks.

Word to the Wise

Make sure your pot is deep enough; it should be at least four times as deep as the liquid, measured from the inside of the pot. Do not double recipes or add more liquid than called for. The liquid will likely bubble right to the top of the pot. (It's a real sticky mess to clean up if it flows over … don't ask me how I know! You will lose your hard work and ingredients, too!)

Red Plum Jelly

Red plums give a lot of color to this medium-red jelly. This jelly makes a terrific glaze for fruit flans and tarts such as French Apple Tarts.

Prep time: 30 minutes   •   Cook time: 35 to 40 minutes   •   Makes about 4 half-pint jars

2½ lbs. red plums, pitted and quartered, about
15 large plums

Water to cover

2 TB. lemon juice

3½ cups granulated sugar

In a Dutch oven or large heavy-bottomed pot, place plums in enough water to cover; bring to full boil over high heat. Reduce heat to medium; cover and cook for about 25 minutes or until very soft. Mash with a potato masher after about 20 minutes to break up further.

Pour through prepared jelly bag; allow to drip without squeezing.

Measure exactly 4 cups liquid (add water if not enough liquid); pour into the Dutch oven. Stir in lemon juice.

Stir in sugar over medium heat until dissolved. Increase heat to high; bring to full boil, stirring constantly. Boil for 8 to 10 minutes without stirring, until setting point is reached.

Remove from heat; skim off any foam.

Ladle quickly into sterilized jars to within ¼ inch of rim; wipe rims. Apply prepared lids and rings; tighten just until fingertip tight.

Process jars in boiling water canner for five minutes.

Let rest at room temperature until set. Check seals; refrigerate any unsealed jars for up to three weeks.

 Word to the Wise
Be meticulous in skimming the foam off the surface before transferring into jars so that your jelly remains clear.

Rhuberry Jelly

Tangy strawberry-rhubarb flavor with a touch of citrus makes this a refreshing glaze for fruit flans and apple or pear tarts. It's a great early summer jelly. Freeze rhubarb when it is abundant.

Prep time: 40 minutes • Cook time: 20 to 25 minutes • Makes about 6 half-pint jars

6 cups diced rhubarb, in ½-inch pieces

4 cups stemmed and halved strawberries

1½ cups water

1 orange, cut into wedges

1 (1¼ oz.) pkg. powdered fruit pectin

2 TB. lemon juice

5½ cups granulated sugar

In a Dutch oven or large heavy-bottomed pot, mix together rhubarb, strawberries, and water. Squeeze juice from orange wedges into pot; add wedges to pot. Bring to full boil over high heat. Reduce heat to medium; cover and cook for 15 minutes or until very soft. Use a potato masher to further break down fruit after about 10 minutes.

Pour through prepared jelly bag; allow to drip without squeezing.

Measure exactly 4 cups juice; pour into the Dutch oven. Stir in pectin and lemon juice; bring to full boil over high heat, stirring constantly.

Stir in sugar. Return to full boil, stirring constantly; boil hard for one minute, stirring constantly.

Fruitful Trivia
Rhubarb is actually a vegetable, but because it is usually sweetened, it is thought of as a fruit.

Remove from heat; skim off any foam.

Ladle quickly into sterilized jars to within ¼ inch of rim; wipe rims. Apply prepared lids and rings; tighten just until fingertip tight.

Process jars in boiling water canner for five minutes.

Let rest at room temperature until set. Check seals; refrigerate any unsealed jars for up to three weeks.

The Least You Need to Know

- Don't squeeze the jelly bag, or the jelly will be cloudy.
- Measure the exact amount of juice and sugar so you get the correct balance with the amount of pectin and get a good set.
- Stir sugar in well as jellies are prone to crystallization.
- Learn how to test for setting point to achieve proper consistency and of jelly.
- Work quickly when getting jellies, as some set quickly.

Notes

Notes

Chapter 8

Savory Jellies

In This Chapter

- What is a savory jelly
- Tips for expert ease with savory jellies
- What to do to prevent or fix errors
- Learn about herb, wine, and pepper jellies

Savory jellies are sparkling-clear gels made with wine, vinegar, juice, or water, and sugar, and they are cooked, usually with added pectin; they hold their shape but are tender enough to quiver and spread easily. They include pepper jellies, wine jellies, and herb jellies.

Savory jellies make a wonderful addition to our eating. They can really perk up the flavor of a meal. They make great appetizers (for example, red and green pepper jelly served over cream cheese), are condiments to meats (such as garlic jelly, mint jelly, rosemary jelly, and wine jellies), and act as special flavor ingredients (such as garlic jelly, purple basil wine jelly, or lavender jelly) for fruit and salad dressings, as meat or vegetable glazes, and in sauces.

Hot or sweet pepper jellies have bits of pepper suspended in a clear jelly, so are classified as jellies. Also included here are recipes for garlic jelly, wine jellies, and herb jellies; I have used purple basil, rosemary, mint, and lavender. (The Rosemary Apple-Cider Jelly was the first jelly to win a first-place ribbon at the fair, and I cannot eat chicken without it now!)

Savory jellies are great for gift-giving. You will find some pretty unique jellies in this chapter. Not only will your gift be homemade, it will be something they cannot get just anywhere! (Be careful whom you give them to because I find my friends come back with the empty jar looking for more!) As they are not eaten in the same amounts as regular jellies, I prefer to use the smaller (4-ounce) jelly jars when giving as gifts. See Appendix B for decorating jars and gift-giving ideas.

Testing, One, Two ...

Jams were tested for sugar content using a refractometer, so no more sugar was added than was needed for a good set. A refractometer has a delicate prism inside of it. A little of the preserve is placed on its small glass surface. It is held up to the light, and when you look through the eye piece (which looks like a six-inch telescope) the percentage of sugar present shows up on a scale.

Acidity was also tested with a pH meter to ensure sufficient acid for gelling.

Word to the Wise

Please review Chapter 1 to reacquaint yourself with preserve-making. Things may have changed since you first started making preserves. If you are a beginner, there are a few important things to know before getting started. Many instructions are common to all preserves so, once you get it right for one, you'll sail through the others. It's a lot easier than you might think.

Tips for Prizewinning Jellies

Stop here before beginning to cook for tips on how to get expert results.

- Use only the exact amount of liquid specified in the recipe; using extra may result in a jelly that does not set.

- Measure sugar accurately and stir well to ensure that it is completely dissolved, scraping down any that gets on the sides of the pot or spoon handle. Heating the liquid a little before stirring in the sugar will help the sugar dissolve more quickly.

- Jellies require a full boil. Make sure your pot is deep enough; it should be at least four times as deep as the liquid, measured from the inside of the pot. Do not double recipes or add more liquid than called for. The liquid will likely bubble right to the top of the pot. I recommend using the deepest pot you have or, if you make jellies often, investing in a deeper one—six-inch or deeper, with at least a nine-inch inside diameter. Sticky jelly makes a real mess and can cause burns!

♦ The timing for pectin-added jellies should be exact; use a timer. Check the expiration date on the box of pectin before beginning.

♦ Skim foam from the top of jelly using a large metal spoon (not all jellies will have foam). I do not like to add butter to my jellies, to prevent foaming. To remove small bits of foam that sink or are hard to get, pour through a fine-mesh strainer.

♦ Work quickly with jellies, as they may set quickly. A tip is to pour them from the pot into a sterilized 4 cup glass measure, then pour mixture quickly into jars. If it begins to set, you may get small bubbles in your jelly.

♦ Do not seal jellies with paraffin wax. This practice is no longer considered safe. Do not invert jars after sealing. Process for good seal.

> **Word to the Wise**
>
> To prevent floating, pepper jellies benefit from being stirred for five to seven minutes before ladling into jars. This allows the mixture to cool a bit and begin to thicken, so that the peppers start to suspend. If you rush this step, all the pepper bits will migrate to the top of the jar.

Troubleshooting Tips and Quick Fixes

In this section, you will find practical tips and information on how to fix or prevent some of the common jelly-making errors. A quick read through them may help save problems later. Jellies can sometimes become too soft and runny or too stiff and gluey. Hopefully yours will turn out just right. Here you will also learn how to prevent floating when making pepper jellies, prevent bubbles and crystal formation.

Problem: Jelly does not set or is soft.

Some jellies set as soon as they are cooled, while others may take up to 24 hours or longer. Check the expiration date on the pectin box. You might want to contact the manufacturer of the pectin, using the toll-free number or website on the box; they may have a solution to try for their particular product.

Problem: Jelly is stiff or tough.

This can occur when too much pectin is added. It is likely it was overcooked. Use a timer to time accurately.

Word to the Wise _____
Read through the entire recipe before beginning, even if you have made it before. Make sure to add ingredients in the order given.

Problem: Jelly weeps.

This occurs when liquid seeps from the jelly. Weeping is caused by too much acid in the juice, not enough pectin, or storage of jelly in a place that is too warm or has temperature fluctuations.

Problem: Jelly has small bubbles.

Some jellies begin to set very quickly. If they do, you may get small air bubbles trapped in your jelly. Work quickly, keeping everything hot, and pour mixture quickly into jars.

Problem: Jelly has crystals.

This can occur when too much sugar has been added (may have been measured inaccurately) or when there is undissolved sugar on the sides of the pan or spoon handle. Stir well during cooking and scrape down sides with rubber scraper, if necessary. Crystallization may result from overcooking or from storing jelly in a place that is too warm or has temperature fluctuations.

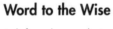

Word to the Wise _____

I define the cook time at the beginning of each recipe as the overall "estimated" cooking time to heat and bring mixtures to a boil as well as the boiling or simmering time specified in the recipe. With preserving (vs. other regular cooking recipes) the time will vary with the type of pot used (metal, glass, size) and how often it is stirred, etc.

Garlic Jelly

Using a food processor makes finely mincing the large amount of garlic an easy task. Serve this jelly with cream cheese on crackers. Use it to glaze roast chicken or to make Garlic Chicken Portobello. If desired, place a sprig of rosemary in jar before adding jelly.

Prep time: 20 minutes   •   Cook time: 15 to 20 minutes   •   Makes about 4 half-pint jars or 8 (4 oz.) jelly jars

2 cups apple juice, white wine, or water

1 cup cider vinegar or white wine vinegar

¼ cup finely minced garlic

4 cups granulated sugar

1 pouch (3 oz.) liquid fruit pectin

In a Dutch oven or large heavy-bottomed pot, mix together apple juice, vinegar, and garlic; bring to full boil over high heat. Reduce heat; cover and simmer for five minutes. Measure 2½ cups (adding water if needed) and return to pot.

Stir in sugar; bring to full boil over high heat, stirring constantly.

Stir in pectin; return to full boil. Boil hard for one minute, stirring constantly.

Remove from heat; stir for five minutes (this prevents floating garlic, although some garlic may settle to the bottom as it cools).

Ladle into prepared jars to within ¼ inch of rim; wipe rims. Apply prepared lids and rings; tighten just until fingertip tight.

Process jars in boiling water canner for five minutes.

Let rest at room temperature until set. Check seals; refrigerate any unsealed jars for up to three weeks.

Fruitful Trivia
Whole garlic is called a head while the individual sections are called cloves. Choose garlic that is firm and whose outer papery covering is intact. Avoid any that are sprouting and store in a cool, dry, dark place.

Red and Green Pepper Jelly

This attractive jelly with suspended bits of red and green sweet peppers is great served over cream cheese on crackers as an appetizer or snack. This recipe can also be made with all red or all green peppers. If you follow these instructions, then you should have no problem with floating peppers. Hot pepper jellies are very popular and make great Christmas or host/hostess gifts.

Prep time: 30 minutes • Cook time: 25 to 30 minutes • Makes about 5 half-pint jars or 10 (4 oz.) jelly jars

1 cup finely chopped red bell peppers

1 cup finely chopped green bell peppers

1 to 2 jalapeño peppers, minced (optional)

1½ cups cider vinegar

½ tsp. hot pepper sauce, or ¼ tsp. hot red chili-pepper flakes

6½ cups granulated sugar

2 (3 oz.) pouches liquid fruit pectin

In a Dutch oven or large heavy-bottomed pot, stir together red and green bell peppers, jalapeño peppers, vinegar, hot pepper sauce, and sugar. Bring to full boil over medium heat, stirring constantly; boil gently for five minutes. Remove from heat, and let stand for 20 minutes, stirring occasionally.

Return to full boil over high heat, stirring constantly.

Immediately stir in pectin; return to full boil. Boil hard one minute, stirring constantly.

Fruitful Trivia

To test for floating, fill one jar; let rest for one minute. If peppers look as if they are starting to float up, pour jelly back into pot and keep stirring; begin again with new sterilized jar.

Remove from heat; skim off any foam. Stir for five to eight minutes (this prevents floating peppers).

Ladle into prepared jars to within ¼ inch of rim; wipe rims. Apply prepared lids and rings; tighten just until fingertip tight.

Process jars in boiling water canner for five minutes.

Let rest at room temperature until set. Check seals; refrigerate any unsealed jars for up to three weeks.

Fire and Ice Jelly (Hot Pepper and Ice Wine Jelly)

This is a sensational jelly made with trendy ice wine. Turn up the heat to suit your own taste with additional hot chili-pepper flakes or cayenne pepper. Serve over cream cheese and crackers, brush over roasted chicken to glaze, or spread on a roast chicken or turkey sandwich.

Prep time: 15 minutes • Cook time: 5 to 10 minutes • Makes about 7 (4 oz.) jelly jars

¾ cup minced red bell pepper

1¼ cup ice wine or sweet dessert wine

4 TB. lemon juice

2 tsp. hot red chili-pepper flakes

3½ cups granulated sugar

1 (3 oz.) pouch liquid fruit pectin

In a Dutch oven or large heavy-bottomed pot, mix together red peppers, wine, lemon juice, pepper flakes, and sugar. Bring to full boil over high heat, stirring constantly; boil hard for one minute. Remove from heat; let stand for 20 minutes, stirring occasionally.

Return to full boil over high heat, stirring constantly.

Immediately stir in pectin; return to full boil. Boil hard for one minute, stirring constantly.

Remove from heat; skim off any foam. Stir for five to seven minutes (this prevents floating peppers).

Ladle into sterilized jars to within ¼ inch of rim; wipe rims. Apply prepared lids and rings; tighten just until fingertip tight.

Process jars in boiling water canner for five minutes.

Let rest at room temperature until set. Check seals; refrigerate any unsealed jars for up to three weeks.

Fruitful Trivia _____

Ice wine is made from pressing frozen grapes to extract the sweet nectar. It is sold in small bottles and, although it is a bit pricey, the distinctive flavor is unmatched. True ice wines are made from grapes naturally frozen on the vine, while others are made from artificially frozen grapes.

Cabernet Wine Jelly

Although a Cabernet wine was used for this jelly, you might want to choose a wine to match the one you are planning to serve for a special occasion. Reserving some of the wine to add after the sugar is dissolved helps to retain the flavor of the wine.

Prep time: 5 minutes • Cook time: 10 to 15 minutes • Makes about 7 (4 oz.) jelly jars

3¼ cups granulated sugar

2 cups Cabernet wine, or any other red or white wine

1 (3 oz.) pouch liquid fruit pectin

In a Dutch oven or large heavy-bottomed pot, mix together sugar and 1 cup wine. Cook over medium-high heat; when almost boiling, add remaining 1 cup wine. Bring to full boil over high heat, stirring occasionally.

Immediately stir in pectin; return to full boil. Boil hard for one minute, stirring constantly.

Word to the Wise

When cooking with wine, use table wine, not cooking wine—always use the same kind of wine to cook with that you would drink, to get the best flavor!

Remove from heat; let stand for one minute. Skim off any foam.

Ladle into sterilized jars to within ¼ inch of rim; wipe rims. Apply prepared lids and rings; tighten just until fingertip tight.

Process jars in boiling water canner for five minutes.

Let rest at room temperature until set. Check seals; refrigerate any unsealed jars for up to three weeks.

Spiced Cranberry and Red Wine Jelly

This beautifully colored jelly is lightly spiced with cinnamon, cloves, and nutmeg. Serve as a condiment with Thanksgiving and Christmas turkeys, chicken, or pork chops.

Prep time: 10 minutes • Cook time: 10 to 15 minutes • Makes about 7 (4 oz.) jelly jars

3¼ cups granulated sugar

1 cup sweetened cranberry juice

1 tsp. ground cinnamon

½ tsp. ground cloves

¼ tsp. ground nutmeg

1 cup red wine

1 (3 oz.) pouch liquid fruit pectin

In a Dutch oven or large heavy-bottomed pot, mix together sugar, cranberry juice, cinnamon, cloves, and nutmeg. Cook over medium-high heat; when almost boiling, add wine. Bring to full boil, stirring occasionally.

Immediately stir in pectin; return to full boil. Boil hard for one minute, stirring constantly.

Remove from heat; let stand for one minute. Skim off any foam.

Ladle into sterilized jars to within ¼ inch of rim; wipe rims. Apply prepared lids and rings; tighten just until fingertip tight.

Process jars in boiling water canner for five minutes.

Let rest at room temperature until set. Check seals; refrigerate any unsealed jars for up to three weeks.

Word to the Wise
Sterilizing jars means to boil cleaned jars in a boiling water canner for 10 minutes, beginning timing once water begins to boil. This kills any microorganisms and heats the jars for filling with hot jelly. Leave sterilized jars in hot water until ready to fill.

Spiced Port Wine Jelly

Delicious served over cream cheese and crackers, and served along with peppercorn pâté.

Prep time: 10 minutes • Cook time: 10 to 15 minutes • Makes about 7 (4 oz.) jelly jars

3¼ cups granulated sugar

2 cups port wine

¼ tsp. ground cinnamon

Pinch ground cloves

Pinch nutmeg

1 (3 oz.) pouch liquid fruit pectin

In a Dutch oven or large heavy-bottomed pot, mix together sugar, 1 cup wine, cinnamon, cloves, and nutmeg. Cook over medium-high heat; when almost boiling, add remaining 1 cup wine. Bring to full boil, stirring occasionally.

Immediately stir in pectin; return to full boil. Boil hard for one minute, stirring constantly.

Remove from heat; let stand for one minute. Skim off any foam.

Fruitful Trivia
Port is a perfect ingredient for jelly—it is a sweet, fortified wine, often with a very fruity taste.

Ladle into sterilized jars to within ¼ inch of rim; wipe rims. Apply prepared lids and rings; tighten just until fingertip tight.

Process jars in boiling water canner for five minutes.

Let rest at room temperature until set. Check seals; refrigerate any unsealed jars for up to three weeks.

Sangria Jelly

This fruity wine jelly closely resembles the taste of the delicious drink it is named after. Serve over cream cheese on crackers.

Prep time: 10 minutes   •   Cook time: 10 to 15 minutes   •   Makes about 4 half-pint jars or 8 (4 oz.) jelly jars

1½ cups dry full-bodied red wine, such as Burgundy or Cabernet

¾ cup orange juice

2 TB. lemon or lime juice

3¼ cups granulated sugar

1 (3 oz.) pouch liquid fruit pectin

2 TB. brandy or orange liqueur

In a Dutch oven or large heavy-bottomed pot, mix together wine, orange juice, lemon juice, and sugar; bring to full boil over high heat, stirring constantly.

Immediately stir in pectin; return to a full boil. Boil hard for one minute, stirring constantly.

Remove from heat; stir in brandy. Skim off any foam.

Ladle into sterilized jars to within ¼ inch of rim; wipe rims. Apply prepared lids and rings; tighten just until fingertip tight.

Process jars in boiling water canner for five minutes.

Let rest at room temperature until set. Check seals; refrigerate any unsealed jars for up to three weeks.

Well Defined

Sangria (pronounced *san-GREE-ah*) is the Spanish word for "blood"; it refers to the deep red color of the drink and the jelly.

Wine and Roses Jelly

This attractive jelly, with rose petals suspended in a clear pink jelly, makes a wonderful gift. Serve it with Cream Tea Scones to appreciate its delicate flavor and fragrance. Tastes lovely brushed over a fruit flan or tart.

Prep time: 15 minutes   •   Cook time: 10 to 15 minutes   •   Makes about 4 half-pint jars or 8 (4 oz.) jelly jars

2½ cups organically grown pink or red rose petals (white or yellow tips removed from pointed end where they attach to stem), lightly packed

3 cups white wine, sparkling wine or champagne, or 3 cups water

2 TB. lemon juice

3½ cups granulated sugar

1 (3 oz.) pouch liquid fruit pectin

To make infusion: In a Dutch oven or large heavy-bottomed pot, mix together 2 cups rose petals (reserve ½ cup for later) and the wine or water; bring to a full boil over high heat. Reduce heat; cover and simmer for five minutes. Strain, reserving liquid; squeeze petals and discard.

Add lemon juice to liquid; add enough water to measure exactly 2½ cups. Return infused liquid to pot.

Stir in sugar; bring to full boil over high heat, stirring constantly.

Fast Lane _____

To get rose petals to properly suspend in the jelly, add petals to the jelly mixture in a sterilized, large glass measure and stir slowly with a sterilized skewer until they look like they will stay suspended; then pour mixture into jars. (It's hard to tell when they are in the pot.)

Immediately stir in pectin; return to full boil. Boil hard for one minute, stirring constantly.

Remove from heat; skim off any foam. Stir in remaining ½ cup rose petals; stir slowly for 5 minutes (this prevents floating petals).

Ladle into sterilized jars to within ¼ inch of rim; wipe rims. Apply prepared lids and rings; tighten just until fingertip tight.

Process jars in boiling water canner for five minutes.

Let rest at room temperature until set. Check seals; refrigerate any unsealed jars for up to three weeks.

Word to the Wise

Use only roses that have not been sprayed with pesticides or insecticides. You may use roses you grow yourself, but not commercial roses.

Strawberry Fields Wine Jelly

Wines made from fruit (not fruit-flavored wines) are growing in popularity. They are great to use for wine jellies. This jelly was named after a wine produced by a local berry grower.

Prep time: 5 minutes • Cook time: 10 to 15 minutes • Makes about 9 (4 oz.) jelly jars

3 cups strawberry wine or other fruit wine

4¼ cups granulated sugar

1 (3 oz.) pouch liquid fruit pectin

In a Dutch oven or large heavy-bottomed pot, mix together wine and sugar; bring to a full boil over high heat, stirring constantly.

>
> ### Word to the Wise
> Preserves are sealed when the lids curve inward. Test seal by pressing in center—if lid moves, then it has not sealed, so refrigerate immediately. For stored preserves, discard anywhere the lids have popped up.

Immediately stir in pectin; return to a full boil. Boil hard for one minute, stirring constantly.

Remove from heat; skim off any foam.

Ladle into sterilized jars to within ¼ inch of rim; wipe rims. Apply prepared lids and rings; tighten just until fingertip tight.

Process jars in boiling water canner for five minutes.

Let rest at room temperature until set. Check seals; refrigerate any unsealed jars for up to three weeks.

Purple Basil Wine Jelly

Purple basil (also opal basil or purple ruffles) has deep-reddish-purple leaves. When infused in white wine, the wine turns a beautiful red. This herb jelly smells sweetly of basil, yet the flavor is subtler than Italian green basil.

Prep time: 15 minutes   •   Cook time: 10 to 15 minutes   •   Makes about 4 half-pint jars or 8 (4 oz.) jelly jars

3 cups dry white wine

1½ cups purple basil leaves, loosely packed

1 TB. white wine vinegar

4 cups granulated sugar

1 (3 oz.) pouch liquid fruit pectin

To make infused wine: In a Dutch oven or large heavy-bottomed pot, bring wine to a full boil over high heat; stir in basil leaves. Reduce heat; cover and simmer for five minutes. Remove from heat; let steep for five minutes. Strain, reserving liquid; squeeze leaves and discard.

Add enough water to liquid to measure exactly 3 cups. Return infused wine to the Dutch oven.

Stir in vinegar and sugar; bring to full boil over high heat, stirring constantly.

Immediately stir in pectin; return to full boil. Boil hard for one minute, stirring constantly.

Remove from heat; skim off any foam.

Ladle into sterilized jars to within ¼ inch of rim; wipe rims. Apply prepared lids and rings; tighten just until fingertip tight.

Process jars in boiling water canner for five minutes.

Let rest at room temperature until set. Check seals; refrigerate any unsealed jars for up to three weeks.

Lavender Jelly

This jelly has a beautiful mauve color and a delicate flavor, scented with lavender. Try it on scones, stir it into fresh fruit, or use it to glaze a fruit flan or an open fruit tart. Goes well with lemon, orange, apple, peach, strawberry, raspberry, and blueberry.

Prep time: 10 minutes • Cook time: 30 to 35 minutes • Makes about 5 (4 oz.) jelly jars

4 cups water

1 cup fresh lavender blossom clusters

¼ cup lemon juice

1 (1¾ oz.) pkg. powdered fruit pectin

5⅔ cups granulated sugar

To make lavender infusion: In a Dutch oven or large heavy-bottomed pot, mix together water and lavender; bring to full boil over high heat. Reduce heat; cover and simmer for 20 minutes. Strain, reserving liquid; squeeze flowers and discard.

Measure exactly 2½ cups infused liquid; return to the Dutch oven. Stir in lemon juice and pectin. Bring to full boil over high heat, stirring constantly.

Stir in sugar; return to full boil over high heat, stirring constantly. Boil hard for one minute, stirring constantly.

Remove from heat; skim off any foam.

Ladle into sterilized jars to within ¼ inch of rim; wipe rims. Apply prepared lids and rings; tighten just until fingertip tight.

Process jars in boiling water canner for five minutes.

Let rest at room temperature until set. Check seals; refrigerate any unsealed jars for up to three weeks.

Lemon Verbena Jelly

This clear, lemony herb jelly goes well with chicken, pork, veal, or lamb, served alongside or as a glaze. Stir into sauces made from pan drippings. It is also tasty on biscuits, as a glaze for fruit flans or tarts, or stirred into clear hot tea.

Prep time: 10 minutes   •   Cook time: 15 to 20 minutes   •   Makes about 3 half-pint jars or 6 (4 oz.) jelly jars

3 cups water

1½ cups torn *lemon verbena* leaves, lightly packed

2 TB. lemon juice

1 (1¼ oz.) pkg. powdered fruit pectin

3 cups granulated sugar

To make infusion: In a Dutch oven or large heavy-bottomed pot, mix together water and lemon verbena leaves; bring to full boil over high heat. Reduce heat; cover and simmer for five minutes. Strain, reserving liquid; squeeze leaves and discard.

Measure exactly 2½ cups infused liquid; return to the Dutch oven. Stir in lemon juice and pectin. Bring to full boil over high heat, stirring constantly.

Stir in sugar; return to full boil over high heat, stirring constantly. Boil hard for one minute, stirring constantly.

Remove from heat; skim off any foam.

Ladle into sterilized jars to within ¼ inch of rim; wipe rims. Apply prepared lids and rings; tighten just until fingertip tight.

Process jars in boiling water canner for five minutes.

Let rest at room temperature until set. Check seals; refrigerate any unsealed jars for up to three weeks.

Well Defined _____

Lemon verbena is a tender perennial herb with long pointed leaves and an exquisite lemon flavor. You can find seedlings in your local nursery to grow; it thrives in full sun. It is excellent for jelly-making, also great steeped for tea.

Mint Jelly

This is a classic mint jelly, typically served with lamb. I usually make it with spearmint but it may be made with any variety of mints.

Prep time: 15 minutes • Cook time: 15 to 20 minutes • Makes about 4 half-pint jars or 8 (4 oz.) jelly jars

2½ cups water

2 cups whole mint leaves, loosely packed (see the following Fruitful Trivia sidebar)

¾ cup cider vinegar

1 (1¼ oz.) pkg. powdered fruit pectin

4 cups granulated sugar

½ cup finely chopped mint leaves (optional)

Green food coloring (optional)

To make infusion: In a Dutch oven or large heavy-bottomed pot, mix together water and 2 cups whole mint leaves; bring to a boil over high heat. Reduce heat; cover and simmer for 15 minutes. Strain, reserving liquid; squeeze leaves and discard.

Measure exactly 2 cups infused liquid; return to the Dutch oven. Stir in vinegar and pectin. Bring to full boil over high heat, stirring constantly.

Stir in sugar; return to full boil over high heat, stirring constantly. Boil hard for one minute, stirring constantly.

Remove from heat; skim off any foam. Stir in ½ cup chopped mint leaves and food coloring, if using; stir slowly for five minutes (this prevents floating leaves).

Fruitful Trivia

There is a wide variety of mints available that can be used to make jelly, such as peppermint, spearmint, apple mint, pineapple mint, lemon mint, orange mint, and even chocolate mint. Look for them in your local nursery and grow your own. If possible, plant in containers, as mint will spread in the garden. Mint thrives in moist, well-drained soil and partial sun.

Ladle into sterilized jars to within ¼ inch of rim; wipe rims. Apply prepared lids and rings; tighten just until fingertip tight.

Process jars in boiling water canner for five minutes.

Let rest at room temperature until set. Check seals; refrigerate any unsealed jars for up to three weeks.

Pineapple and Mint Jelly

To make this jelly, pineapple juice is first infused with mint. Then, at the end of the cooking, additional mint is stirred in, producing a light-yellow jelly with suspended bits of fresh mint. Serve on scones or with lamb.

Prep time: 20 minutes • Cook time: 15 to 20 minutes • Makes about 5 half-pint jars

4 cups unsweetened pineapple juice

1 cup chopped fresh mint leaves, loosely packed (see Mint Jelly)

2 TB. lemon juice

1 (1¼ oz.) pkg. powdered fruit pectin

4 cups granulated sugar

2 TB. finely chopped fresh mint

To make infused juice: In a Dutch oven or large heavy-bottomed pot, mix together pineapple juice and the 1 cup chopped mint leaves; bring to full boil over high heat. Reduce heat; cover and simmer for five minutes. Strain, reserving liquid; squeeze leaves and discard.

Measure exactly 3¾ cups infused juice; return to the Dutch oven. Stir in lemon juice and pectin. Bring to full boil over high heat, stirring constantly.

Stir in sugar; return to full boil over high heat, stirring constantly. Boil hard for one minute, stirring constantly.

Remove from heat; skim off any foam. Stir in the 2 tablespoons finely chopped mint; stir for eight minutes (this will prevent floating mint).

Fast Lane
To save time, use your food processor to chop mint.

Ladle into sterilized jars to within ¼ inch of rim; wipe rims. Apply prepared lids and rings; tighten just until fingertip tight.

Process jars in boiling water canner for five minutes.

Let rest at room temperature until set. Check seals; refrigerate any unsealed jars for up to three weeks.

Rosemary Apple Cider Jelly

This jelly earned me my first red ribbon for first prize at the local fair. It is still one of my favorite jellies and one I have frequent requests for. Serve this savory jelly with roasted chicken, lamb, or pork, or brush over top in the last 10 minutes of cooking. For gift-giving, place a small sprig of fresh rosemary in each jar before pouring in the jelly.

Prep time: 20 minutes   •   Cook time: 10 to 15 minutes   •   Makes about 4 half-pint jars

2½ cups apple cider

⅓ cup coarsely chopped fresh rosemary, loosely packed

2 TB. cider vinegar or lemon juice

3½ cups granulated sugar

1 (3 oz.) pouch liquid fruit pectin

To make infused cider: In a Dutch oven or large heavy-bottomed pot, mix together apple cider and rosemary; bring to a full boil over high heat. Reduce heat and simmer for 20 minutes. Strain, reserving liquid; squeeze leaves and discard.

Measure infused cider, adding additional cider or water, to measure exactly 2¼ cups. Return infused cider to the Dutch oven.

Stir in vinegar and sugar; bring to full boil over high heat, stirring constantly.

Immediately stir in pectin; return to full boil. Boil hard for one minute, stirring constantly.

Remove from heat; skim off any foam.

Ladle into prepared jars to within ¼ inch of rim; wipe rims. Apply prepared lids and rings; tighten rings just until fingertip tight.

Process jars in boiling water canner for five minutes.

Let rest at room temperature until set. Check seals; refrigerate any unsealed jars for up to three weeks.

Variation

Cranberry Rosemary Jelly: Substitute cranberry juice for the apple cider.

Fruitful Trivia

Rosemary grows wild in the Mediterranean area. It has silvery green needlelike leaves with an aromatic pine-lemon scent.

The Least You Need to Know

- ◆ You can use savory jellies to enhance meals and recipes.
- ◆ Wine jellies are easy and quick to make because preparation is minimal.
- ◆ Infusing liquids with the flavor of fresh herbs can make fabulous jellies.
- ◆ You can prevent peppers from floating in pepper jellies by stirring for five to eight minutes after you skim off the foam. This allows the mixture to cool a bit and begin to thicken, so that the peppers start to suspend.

Notes

Notes

Chapter 9

Marmalades

In This Chapter

- ◆ What is a marmalade?
- ◆ Tips for expert ease with marmalades
- ◆ What to do to prevent or fix errors

Marmalades are spreads made with one or more citrus fruit, or with citrus and other fruit or vegetable, using fruit pulp/juice and citrus rind; they are cooked with sugar, are set with naturally present pectin or added commercial pectin, and small pieces of fruit or citrus rind are suspended in a transparent jelly.

The word *marmalade* comes from Portuguese "marmelo," meaning quince, popular for jelly-making prior to the use of citrus fruit because of its high level of pectin. Marmalade is known for a bitter-tart flavor derived from the inclusion of grated, finely chopped or sliced citrus rind. It was a British family who first started adding strips of orange rind to jam and jelly.

In this collection are recipes for some of your favorites, such as Lime and Seville Orange marmalades, as well as interesting combinations with cranberry, peach, carrot, or zucchini. Some recipes use finely grated rind and will appeal to those who find traditional marmalade too heavy with thick rind. I have used sweet seedless oranges, whose rinds soften with little cooking. Most recipes have been simplified to be as easy as possible. Seville Orange Marmalade, a classic, does take a bit more work and is made in January when Seville oranges are available.

> ### Word to the Wise
>
> Please review Chapter 1 to reacquaint yourself with preserve-making. Things may have changed since you first started making preserves. If you are a beginner, there are a few important things to know before getting started. Many instructions are common to all preserves so, once you get it right for one, you'll sail through the others. It's a lot easier than might think.

Testing, One, Two ...

Marmalades were tested for sugar content using a refractometer so that no more sugar was added than was needed for a good set. A refractometer has a delicate prism inside of it. A little of the preserve is placed on its small glass surface. It is held up to the light and when you look through the eye piece (which looks like a six-inch telescope) the percentage of sugar present shows up on a scale.

Acidity was also tested with a pH meter to ensure sufficient acid for gelling.

Tips for Prizewinning Marmalades

Stop here before beginning to cook for tips on how to get expert results:

- Scrub citrus fruit well with warm soapy water; rinse well. Be meticulous in your preparation of the fruit, particularly in the cutting of the rinds to achieve thin, even pieces. Make sure your knife is sharp.
- Measure carefully. When adding the sugar, stir well to ensure that it is completely dissolved, scraping down any that gets on the sides of the pot or spoon handle. Undissolved sugar can crystallize in your marmalade. Heating the fruit a little before stirring in the sugar will help the sugar to dissolve more quickly.
- Stir and watch your marmalade; pectin-added marmalades require a full boil, constantly stirred. Marmalades with natural pectin will thicken as they cook, so stir constantly to prevent scorching. A large, wide diameter pot is recommended to allow the mixture to evaporate more quickly and retain better color and flavor.

- The timing for pectin-added marmalades should be exact; use a timer. Check expiration date on the box of pectin before beginning. Do not interchange liquid pectin and crystals in recipes. Mix in pectin well.

- For marmalades without added pectin, timing will vary, depending on the amount of pectin in the fruit and peels, how well you measure, how fruit is chopped or sliced, and the diameter of your pot. These marmalades must be tested to determine when they have reached the setting point. Be sure to leave in the freezer long enough for the marmalade to cool and to give an idea of the set. Do not put too much on the plate, just a teaspoonful. Always remove the pot from heat to stop cooking the marmalade.

Word to the Wise

Marmalades may take a little longer to set than some jams after they have cooled, particularly those made without added pectin. Let rest without disturbing for about one week.

- To prevent floating of the fruit pieces, stir slowly for about seven minutes after removing from heat.

- Skim any foam using a large metal spoon. (Not all marmalades will have foam.)

Troubleshooting Tips and Quick Fixes

In this section, you will find practical tips and information on how to fix or prevent some of the common marmalade-making errors. A quick read through them may help save problems later. Marmalades can sometimes become too soft and runny or too stiff and gluey. Hopefully yours will turn out just right. Learn also how to prevent tough or floating rind.

Problem: Marmalade does not set, or is thin and runny.

Marmalades may take up to a week to set. Let rest undisturbed. If your marmalade does not set after this time, check your recipe. If it is a pectin-added recipe, check the expiration date on the pectin box. You might want to contact the manufacturer of the pectin, using the toll-free number or website on the box; they may have a solution to try for their particular product.

For marmalades without added pectin, you may need to cook it a little longer. If the jars have all sealed properly, then the contents are safe. Return marmalade to pot, discard used lids, and begin cooking and testing for setting point. It may only take another couple minutes for it to reach the setting point. Then proceed with sterilized jars and new prepared lids.

Problem: Marmalade is stiff or tough.

This can occur when fruit is high in natural pectin or when too much pectin was added. Likely your marmalade was overcooked. To salvage, dilute it with fruit juice or a little liqueur and warm in microwave to make more spreadable.

Problem: Rind is tough.

Likely rind was not pre-cooked long enough to soften. To salvage, warm marmalade to thin it, and then press through strainer; discard rind (the flavor will still be in the marmalade). Reheat and process, or store in refrigerator.

Word to the Wise

Read through the entire recipe before beginning, even if you have made it before. Make sure to add ingredients in the order given.

Problem: Floating rind.

To prevent floating, stir mixture slowly for about seven minutes after removing from heat. Then pour into first jar, and leave for about 30 seconds. If rind still floats, pour back into pot and stir a minute or two longer. You might want to retest for setting point to ensure it has been cooked long enough.

Word to the Wise

I define the cook time at the beginning of each recipe as the overall "estimated" cooking time to heat and bring mixtures to a boil as well as the boiling or simmering time specified in the recipe. With preserving (vs. other regular cooking recipes) the time will vary with the type of pot used (metal, glass, size) and how often it is stirred, etc.

Carrot Orange Marmalade

This is a fine-textured marmalade with small shreds of carrot, orange, and lemon rind. Serve with bran muffins to give them a lift, or use to make Fruit Loaf or Marmalade Pecan Cookies. Make this marmalade in the winter months when other fruits are out of season.

Prep time: 30 minutes • Cook time: 25 to 30 minutes • Makes about 7 half-pint jars

3 cups finely shredded carrot, about 1 lb. carrots

Finely grated rind and juice from 2 large seedless oranges

Finely grated rind and juice from 3 medium lemons

1 cup water

7 cups granulated sugar

2 (3 oz.) pouches liquid fruit pectin

In a Dutch oven or large heavy-bottomed pot, mix together carrots, orange rind and juice, lemon rind and juice, and water; bring to full boil. Reduce to low heat; cover and simmer for about 15 minutes or until carrots and rind have softened.

Stir in sugar; bring to full boil over high heat, stirring constantly. Boil hard for one minute.

Remove from heat; immediately stir in pectin. Skim off any foam. Stir for five to seven minutes (this will prevent floating fruit and carrots).

Ladle into sterilized jars to within ¼ inch of rim; wipe rims. Apply prepared lids and rings; tighten rings just until fingertip tight.

Process jars in boiling water canner for five minutes.

Let rest at room temperature until set. Check seals; refrigerate any unsealed jars up to three weeks.

Fast Lane

Use a food processor, fitted with a grating attachment, to grate carrots. When new, sweet carrots are in season, grate extra to freeze; store pre-measured quantity in freezer bag, squeezing out excess air.

Cranberry Orange Marmalade

This classic taste combination produces a delicious marmalade that is deep red with lots of orange rind. Use to glaze poultry or to make Fruit Loaf. Place a spoonful on grapefruit halves and warm in a microwave.

Prep time: 25 minutes • Cook time: 15 to 20 minutes • Makes about 5 half-pint jars

4 medium seedless oranges, to make 2⅔ cup juice

1 cup water

2¼ cups frozen cranberry cocktail, thawed, plus 2¼ cups water

3 TB. lemon juice

3½ cups granulated sugar

1 cup fresh or frozen cranberries

Cut oranges in half and juice. Cut in half again and thinly slice rind. Place orange juice, rind, and water in a Dutch oven or large heavy-bottomed pot; bring to boil over high heat. Reduce heat; cover and simmer for about 20 minutes or until rind is softened.

Stir in cranberry cocktail plus water and lemon juice.

Stir in sugar over medium heat until sugar is dissolved. Increase heat to high; bring to full boil, stirring constantly. Boil rapidly for five minutes, stirring often. Stir in cranberries; cook for five to ten minutes longer, until marmalade thickens, stirring often. Test for setting point.

Fast Lane

Pick up a few extra bags of cranberries in the fall when they are in the stores. Place package into a freezer bag and store in the freezer for up to one year. Cranberries are native to the cooler northern areas of North America.

Remove from heat; skim off any foam. Stir for five to seven minutes (this will prevent floating fruit).

Ladle into sterilized jars to within ¼ inch of rim; wipe rims. Apply prepared lids and rings; tighten rings just until fingertip tight.

Process jars in boiling water canner for five minutes.

Let rest at room temperature until set. Check seals; refrigerate any unsealed jars up to three weeks. Marmalade is best served after resting for one week.

Lemon Ginger Marmalade

This is a lovely yellow marmalade with the essence of ginger. Toss a little with cooked green beans to glaze them or, when cooking winter squash, replace the brown sugar with marmalade added to taste. Use to make Fruit Loaf.

Prep time: 35 minutes   •   Cook time: 35 to 40 minutes   •   Makes about 5 half-pint jars

3 large lemons

4½ cups water

4¾ cups granulated sugar

⅓ cup thinly sliced crystallized ginger

Cut lemons in half and juice to measure ¾ cup; place seeds in a small square of cheesecloth. Cut in half again and thinly slice rind. Remove extra pith and place in the cheesecloth with seeds; tie with string. Place rind, juice, water, and cheesecloth bag in a medium saucepan; bring to full boil over high heat. Reduce heat; cover and simmer for 15 to 20 minutes or until rind is softened.

In a Dutch oven or large heavy-bottomed pot, place rind plus liquid. Squeeze and discard cheesecloth bag.

Stir in sugar and ginger over medium heat until sugar is dissolved. Increase heat to high; bring to full boil, stirring constantly. Boil rapidly for 12 to 15 minutes until marmalade thickens, stirring often. Test for setting point.

Remove from heat; skim off any foam. Stir for five to seven minutes (this will prevent floating rind).

Ladle into sterilized jars to within ¼ inch of rim; wipe rims. Apply prepared lids and rings; tighten rings just until fingertip tight.

Process jars in boiling water canner for five minutes.

Let rest at room temperature until set. Check seals; refrigerate any unsealed jars up to three weeks. Marmalade is best served after resting for one week.

Word to the Wise

Scrub citrus fruit well with warm soapy water; rinse well. Be meticulous in your preparation of the fruit, particularly in the cutting of the rinds to achieve thin, even pieces. Make sure your knife is sharp.

Lemon Lime Marmalade

This citrus duo makes a superb-tasting marmalade that is lovely and tart. Use as an ingredient for Lime Phyllo Tarts.

Prep time: 40 minutes • Cook time: 45 to 50 minutes • Makes about 7 half-pint jars

3 medium lemons

4 medium limes

7½ cups water

7 cups granulated sugar

Cut lemons in half and juice to make ¾ cup. Cut limes in half and juice to make ⅔ cup. Place seeds in a small square of cheesecloth. (If limes are dry, you may need more to get enough juice.) Cut in half again and thinly slice rind. Remove extra pith; place in a cheesecloth with seeds; tie with string. Place rind, juice, water, and a cheesecloth bag in a medium saucepan; bring to full boil over high heat. Reduce heat; cover and simmer for 15 to 20 minutes or until rind is softened.

In a Dutch oven or large heavy-bottomed pot, place rind plus liquid. Squeeze and discard cheesecloth bag.

Stir in sugar over medium heat until dissolved. Increase heat to high; bring to full boil, stirring constantly. Boil rapidly for 20 to 25 minutes until marmalade thickens, stirring often. Test for setting point.

Fast Lane

To make a quick sauce for steamed puddings such as Christmas pudding, or to top plain cakes or ice cream, combine ½ cup marmalade and ¼ cup brandy, bourbon, or whisky. Heat in a small saucepan or microwave in a glass bowl, until hot, stirring to blend.

Remove from heat; skim off any foam. Stir for five to seven minutes (this will prevent floating rind).

Ladle into sterilized jars to within ¼ inch of rim; wipe rims. Apply prepared lids and rings; tighten rings just until fingertip tight.

Process jars in boiling water canner for five minutes.

Let rest at room temperature until set. Check seals; refrigerate any unsealed jars up to three weeks. Marmalade is best served after resting for one week.

Lemon and Mint Marmalade with Calendula Petals

This lemony marmalade had a refreshing touch of fresh mint and edible flower petals.

Prep time: 50 minutes • Cook time: 25 to 30 minutes • Makes about 5 half-pint jars

10 lemons

½ cup water

6 cups granulated sugar

1 (3 oz.) pouch liquid fruit pectin

½ cup chopped fresh mint

⅓ cup organically grown yellow or orange calendula petals

Using a vegetable peeler, remove rind from lemons in wide strips; slice thinly to make 1¼ cups.
Juice lemons to make 2 cups. Discard seeds. Place lemon rind, juice, and water in a medium
saucepan; bring to full boil over high heat. Reduce heat; cover and simmer for 15 to 20 minutes
or until rind is softened.

In a Dutch oven or large heavy-bottomed pot, place rind plus liquid.

Stir in sugar; bring to full boil over high heat, stirring constantly. Boil hard for one minute.

Remove from heat; immediately stir in pectin. Skim off any foam. Stir in mint and calendula
petals; stir for five to seven minutes (this will prevent floating).

Ladle into sterilized jars to within ¼ inch of rim; wipe rims. Apply prepared lids and rings;
tighten rings just until fingertip tight.

Process jars in boiling water canner for five minutes.

Let rest at room temperature until set. Check seals;
refrigerate any unsealed jars up to three weeks.

Variations

Lemon Tarragon: Omit the flower petals and substitute
tarragon for the mint.

Lemon Lavender: Omit mint and substitute 2 tablespoons fresh lavender florets for the calendula.

Fruitful Trivia

You may substitute dan-
delion or marigold petals for the
calendula. Ensure that flowers were
not sprayed with herbicides or pesticides. Rinse well to remove any
insects.

Lime Marmalade

This delicious marmalade has the mouth-puckering tartness of a British-style marmalade. Serve with cream cheese on bagels.

Prep time: 50 minutes • Cook time: 40 to 50 minutes • Makes about 5 half-pint jars

10 to 12 large limes

4 cups water

5 cups granulated sugar

Using a vegetable peeler, remove rind from limes in wide strips; slice thinly to make 1½ cups. Juice limes to make 2 cups; discard seeds. Place rind, juice, and water in a medium saucepan; bring to boil over high heat. Reduce heat; cover and simmer for 15 to 20 minutes or until rind is softened.

In a Dutch oven or large heavy-bottomed pot, place rind plus liquid.

Stir in sugar over medium heat until dissolved. Increase heat to high; bring to full boil, stirring constantly. Boil rapidly for 15 to 20 minutes until marmalade thickens, stirring often. Test for setting point.

Remove from heat; skim off any foam. Stir for five to seven minutes (this will prevent floating rind).

Word to the Wise

Do not double recipes. It may overcook fruit or prevent thickening/gelling. And, the pot may boil over even though it doesn't look that full.

Ladle into sterilized jars to within ¼ inch of rim; wipe rims. Apply prepared lids and rings; tighten rings just until fingertip tight.

Process jars in boiling water canner for five minutes.

Let rest at room temperature until set. Check seals; refrigerate any unsealed jars up to three weeks. Marmalade is best served after resting for one week.

Seville Orange Marmalade

Make this classic marmalade in January when Seville oranges are in season. What a great way to start off the new year! Use this marmalade to glaze poultry, or stir into sauces for poultry (after deglazing the pan).

Prep time: 55 minutes • Cook time: 2 hours and 20 minutes • Makes 7 half-pint jars

6 large Seville oranges

Water

Sugar

Cut oranges in half and juice; retain juice but remove seeds and place them in a couple of layers of cheesecloth. Cut oranges in half again. Remove inner membranes and add to cheesecloth; tie with string. Slice orange rind sliver-thin.

Measure combined volume of juice and rind; you should get about 6 cups. Place in a Dutch oven or large heavy-bottomed pot. Add equal volume of water. Place cheesecloth bag into center of the pot; bring to boil over high heat. Reduce heat, and simmer for about two hours or until rind is very soft, stirring occasionally. Squeeze cheesecloth bag several times during cooking.

Measure the rind and liquid; squeeze and discard the cheesecloth bag. Stir in an equal volume of sugar over medium heat until sugar is dissolved. Boil rapidly for 10 to 15 minutes until marmalade thickens, stirring often. Test for setting point.

Remove from heat; skim off any foam. Stir for five to seven minutes (this will prevent floating rind).

Ladle into sterilized jars to within ¼ inch of rim; wipe rims. Apply prepared lids and rings; tighten rings just until fingertip tight.

Process jars in boiling water canner for five minutes.

Let rest at room temperature until set. Check seals; refrigerate any unsealed jars up to three weeks. Marmalade is best served after resting for one week.

Variation

Orange Ginger Marmalade: Use 1 cup thinly sliced crystallized ginger instead of an equal amount of sliced rind.

Scotch (or Spiked!) Marmalade: Stir in 3 tablespoons Scotch whisky, brandy, bourbon, or orange liqueur once set point is reached.

Fruitful Trivia

Seville oranges (grown in the Mediterranean), with their tough, thick skin and bitter, seedy flesh are not eaten fresh, but are perfect for use in classic marmalades, and are used in the making of liqueurs, such as Cointreau, Grand Marnier, and Triple Sec.

Peach Orange Marmalade

Enjoy a wonderful summer peach taste, accented with citrus. If giving it as a gift, you might want to add a little orange liqueur.

Prep time: 50 minutes • Cook time: 25 to 30 minutes • Makes about 8 half-pint jars

1 medium orange

2 medium lemons

2 TB. lemon juice

1 cup water

2 lbs. peeled, pitted, finely chopped peaches, about 8 large

1 (1¾ oz.) pkg. powdered fruit pectin

7 cups granulated sugar

2 TB. orange liqueur (optional)

Cut orange and lemons into quarters; remove seeds and thinly slice or finely chop. Place prepared citrus fruit and any juice, water, and additional lemon juice in a medium saucepan; bring to full boil over high heat. Reduce heat; cover and simmer for 15 to 20 minutes or until rind is softened.

In a Dutch oven or large heavy-bottomed pot, place rind plus liquid and peaches; stir in pectin. Bring to full boil over high heat, stirring constantly.

Stir in sugar; return to full boil. Boil hard for one minute, stirring constantly.

Word to the Wise

Preserves are sealed when lids curve inward. Test seal by pressing in center—if lid moves, then it has not sealed, therefore refrigerate immediately. For stored preserves, discard anywhere the lids have popped up.

Remove from heat; stir in orange liqueur, if using. Skim off any foam. Stir for five to seven minutes (this will prevent floating fruit).

Ladle into sterilized jars to within ¼ inch of rim; wipe rims. Apply prepared lids and rings; tighten rings just until fingertip tight.

Process jars in boiling water canner for five minutes.

Let rest at room temperature until set. Check seals; refrigerate any unsealed jars up to three weeks.

Pineapple Citrus Marmalade

You'll enjoy the refreshing tartness of this bright-colored marmalade. Use as an ingredient for Fried Bananas Caribbean.

Prep time: 40 minutes • Cook time: 35 to 40 minutes • Makes about 6 half-pint jars

2 medium lemons

1 medium orange

1 cup water

4 cups finely chopped fresh pineapple, about 1 medium pineapple

4½ cups granulated sugar

Using a vegetable peeler, remove rind from lemons and orange in wide strips; slice thin. Place rind and water in a medium saucepan; bring to full boil over high heat. Reduce heat; cover and simmer for 15 to 20 minutes or until rind is softened. Section lemons and orange, then remove and discard membranes and seeds; chop flesh.

In a Dutch oven or large heavy-bottomed pot, place rind plus liquid, citrus flesh (plus any juice), and pineapple.

Stir in sugar over medium heat until dissolved. Increase heat to high; bring to full boil, stirring constantly. Boil rapidly for 15 to 20 minutes until marmalade thickens, stirring constantly. Test for setting point.

Remove from heat; skim off any foam. Stir for five to seven minutes (this will prevent floating fruit).

Ladle into sterilized jars to within ¼ inch of rim; wipe rims. Apply prepared lids and rings; tighten rings just until fingertip tight.

Process jars in boiling water canner for five minutes.

Let rest at room temperature until set. Check seals; refrigerate any unsealed jars up to three weeks. Marmalade is best served after resting for one week.

Well Defined

A **canner** is a large pot with a rack deep enough to process jars in boiling water with 1-inch to 2-inch coverage.

Three-Fruit Marmalade (Pink Grapefruit, Lemon, Orange)

This is a classic fruit-trio marmalade with a deep orange color and intense citrus flavor. Use to make Marmalade Pecan Cookies.

Prep time: 45 minutes • Cook time: 60 to 65 minutes • Makes about 7 half-pint jars

2 small pink grapefruit

3 large oranges

4 lemons

4 cups water

7½ cups granulated sugar

Using a vegetable peeler, remove rind from grapefruit, oranges, and lemons in wide strips; slice thin. Line a large wire strainer with several layers of cheesecloth; place over a medium bowl. Juice fruit; pour juice through cheesecloth to catch seeds; place squeezed membranes in cheesecloth with seeds; tie with string.

Place citrus rind (about 3 cups packed), juice (about 3 cups), water, and cheesecloth bag in a Dutch oven or large heavy-bottomed pot; bring to full boil over high heat. Reduce heat; cover and simmer for 25 to 30 minutes or until rind is softened. Squeeze and discard cheesecloth bag.

Fruitful Trivia

Pink grapefruit has more vitamin A than the white type. Grapefruit gets its name from the way it grows—in grapelike clusters. The heavier they are for their size, the more juice grapefruits will have. Store in plastic bag in refrigerator crisper for up to two weeks. Main growing areas are Florida, Arizona, Texas, and California.

Stir in sugar over medium heat until dissolved. Increase heat to high; bring to full boil, stirring constantly. Boil rapidly for 20 to 25 minutes until marmalade thickens, stirring often. Test for setting point.

Remove from heat; skim off any foam. Stir for five to seven minutes (this will prevent floating fruit).

Ladle into sterilized jars to within ¼ inch of rim; wipe rims. Apply prepared lids and rings; tighten rings just until fingertip tight.

Process jars in boiling water canner for five minutes.

Let rest at room temperature until set. Check seals; refrigerate any unsealed jars up to three weeks. Marmalade is best served after resting for one week.

Zucchini Orange Marmalade

This delightful and unusual marmalade is easy to make year round and has an intense, fresh orange flavor. Great for using up the overabundance of zucchini that appears mid-summer!

Prep time: 35 minutes • Cook time: 20 to 30 minutes • Makes about 7 half-pint jars

Finely grated rind of 4 large seedless oranges

2 cups orange juice

4 cups lightly packed shredded zucchini

¼ cup lemon juice

7 cups granulated sugar

2 (3 oz.) pouches liquid fruit pectin

In a small saucepan over medium heat, mix together orange rind and juice; cover and simmer for 10 minutes or until rind is softened. Set aside.

In a Dutch oven or large heavy-bottomed pot over medium heat, cook zucchini, stirring frequently, for five minutes or until softened (water will come out of zucchini as it begins to cook).

Stir in lemon juice, sugar, and reserved orange rind and juice; bring to full boil over high heat, stirring constantly. Boil hard for one minute.

Remove from heat; immediately stir in pectin. Skim off any foam. Stir for seven minutes (this will prevent floating).

Ladle into sterilized jars to within ¼ inch of rim; wipe rims. Apply prepared lids and rings; tighten rings just until fingertip tight.

Process jars in boiling water canner for five minutes.

Let rest at room temperature until set. Check seals; refrigerate any unsealed jars up to three weeks.

Fast Lane

For convenience, use a food processor to shred the zucchini, and a citrus zester to remove rind in shreds.

The Least You Need to Know

- ◆ Citrus fruit has generous amounts of natural pectin in the rind and seeds which causes a good set in marmalades.
- ◆ Be patient when cutting the citrus rind as it is the key to good results.
- ◆ To prevent floating of citrus rind, stir marmalade five to seven minutes before ladling into jars.
- ◆ Marmalades take a bit longer to set than jams. Check set after one week.

Notes

Notes

Fruit Butters

In This Chapter

- ◆ What a fruit butter is
- ◆ Tips for expert ease with fruit butters
- ◆ How to test for doneness
- ◆ What to do to prevent or fix errors

Fruit butters are smooth spreads made from puréed fruit, sugar, and some-times spice, and are slowly cooked down to thicken naturally to a spread-able consistency. They are fairly simple to make and *do not contain any butter*. They are called "butters" for their smooth, buttery consistency. The fruit is often cooked without peeling (which cuts out a lot of work!); then it is pressed through a sieve or is puréed, and is cooked down with sugar and spices until it is thick and spreadable. It's pretty hard to go wrong. The hardest part is the stirring and the time it takes to cook, but even that can be done in two stages. First, cook the fruit and prepare the purée; refrigerate it overnight. Then cook and put into jars the next day.

Most of the fruit butters in this collection were made using apples, so make them when apples are abundant in the fall or when your supply of apples is no longer crunchy. They are also ideal to make when you just have lots of ripe fruit around. The Apricot Orange Butter is made with dried apricots and can be made any time of the year. You can use frozen cranberries and rhubarb to make Cran-Apple and Rhubarb Apple Butters.

Fruit butters have slightly less sugar than other sweet preserves (such as jams, jellies, marmalades, etc.). They will not keep long-term unless processed. Fruit butters are delicious on muffins and toast, or stirred into plain yogurt and topped with crunchy granola.

Word to the Wise

Please review Chapter 1 to reacquaint yourself with preserve-making. Things may have changed since you first started making preserves. If you are a beginner, there are a few important things to know before getting started. Many instructions are common to all preserves so, when you get it right for one, you'll sail through the others. It's a lot easier than you might think.

Tips for Prizewinning Fruit Butters

Stop here before beginning to cook for tips on how to get expert results:

◆ Use ripe fruit; wash well. Overripe fruit can be used as long as it is still in good condition; trim away any very soft parts, bruises, or blemishes. Usually fruit is not peeled or seeded if it is to be put through a strainer or food mill. The recipe will specify to peel and seed if it is to be puréed instead of strained.

◆ Cook fruit until very soft; crush with a potato masher after it has cooked a while to further break down pieces. Stir frequently.

◆ Ensure that there are no lumps of fruit; press through a mesh strainer (sieve) or purée well, according to recipe.

◆ Stir often while the mixture is cooking with the sugar and spices, especially as butter thickens; reduce heat as it thickens but keep it bubbling. Place a wire star underneath pot, if desired, to even out heat and prevent hot spots. The greater the diameter of the pot, the quicker fruit butter will thicken.

◆ Test for doneness (see the following section) when mixture becomes very thick.

◆ Fill jars to within ½ inch from jar rim; process for 10 minutes. Longer processing is required due to lower sugar content than in jams, jellies, and so on.

Test for Doneness

Place a spoonful of fruit butter on a plate. Let stand for a few minutes. It tests done when there is no liquid seeping from the edges. It should be thick enough to mound on a spoon. If you leave some in a small spoon set on a dish to cool, it will set slightly and hold its shape.

Word to the Wise

I define the cook time at the beginning of each recipe as the overall "estimated" cooking time to heat and bring mixtures to a boil as well as the boiling or simmering time specified in the recipe. With preserving (vs. other regular cooking recipes) the time will vary with the type of pot used (metal, glass, size) and how often it is stirred, etc.

Troubleshooting Tips and Quick Fixes

In this section, you will find practical tips and information on how to fix or prevent some of the common fruit butter-making errors. A quick read through them might help save problems later. Butters can sometimes become too soft or too stiff or can scorch while cooking. Hopefully yours will turn out just right.

Word to the Wise

Read through the entire recipe before beginning, even if you have made it before. Make sure to add ingredients in the order given.

Problem: Fruit butter is too soft or liquid seeps from it.

It is likely butter has not been cooked long enough. Continue to cook and test for doneness.

Problem: Fruit butter is stiff.

This can result from overcooking, too much sugar, or insufficient stirring (as the mixture thickens on the bottom of the pot). If it is overcooked, add a little more liquid, such as water or apple cider, and stir well; reheat before canning. If there is too much sugar due to inaccurately measured sugar or fruit, try cooking another apple with a bit of water, press through strainer and add. Remember to stir often and reduce heat to prevent butter from overcooking or scorching on the bottom.

Problem: Fruit butter is sticking (overcooking) on the bottom.

If mixture has not yet scorched, remove from heat and immediately transfer to a clean pot, taking care not to scrape the bottom of the pot. You might need to add a little more liquid if it has thickened too much. Cook over low heat until it tests done. If it has already scorched (it will smell scorched and look very dark on the bottom of the pot), the flavor will have gotten into your butter and the butter will have to be discarded. To prevent scorching, watch mixture carefully and stir often.

Spiced Apple Butter

When you cook this butter, your house will smell like you are baking apple pie. This is a good recipe for using up large quantities of apples, especially when they are no longer crisp.

Prep time: 25 minutes • Cook time: 75 to 80 minutes • Makes about 4 half-pint jars

4 lbs. apples that soften, about 12 medium

1½ cups apple cider

3½ cups packed brown sugar

2 TB. lemon juice

1 tsp. ground cinnamon

¼ tsp. ground nutmeg

¼ tsp. ground cloves

Cut apples into quarters; remove stems and blossom ends. Slice each quarter into four or five slices. Place apples in a Dutch oven or large heavy-bottomed pot; stir in cider. Bring to boil over high heat. Reduce heat; cover and boil gently for about 15 minutes or until apples are very soft.

Ladle fruit and liquid into a mesh strainer and press pulp through; discard peel and seeds. Or extract pulp using a food mill. Return to the clean Dutch oven.

Stir in sugar, lemon juice, cinnamon, nutmeg, and cloves; cook over low heat, stirring constantly, until sugar is dissolved. Increase heat; bring to boil, stirring constantly. Reduce heat; boil gently, uncovered, for about 60 minutes or until thickened. Continue to reduce heat and stir often, especially toward end of cooking time. Test for doneness.

Fruitful Trivia

Make fruit butters containing apples when they have lost their crunch and become soft or when you have a large supply of apples that you want to use up.

Ladle into sterilized jars to within ¼ inch of rim; wipe rims. Apply prepared lids and rings; tighten just until fingertip tight.

Process jars in boiling water canner for 10 minutes.

Let rest at room temperature until cool. Check seals; refrigerate any unsealed jars for up to three weeks.

Apricot Orange Butter

This butter is a perky yellow-orange color with a strong apricot flavor and a refreshing touch of orange. It can be made year around. Some bulk stores carry good quality dried apricots that are very fresh and soft.

Prep time: 25 minutes • Cook time: 45 to 50 minutes • Makes about 5 half-pint jars

4 cups dried apricots

3½ cups water

2⅔ cups granulated sugar

1 TB. finely grated orange rind

⅔ cup orange juice

In a large bowl, place dried apricots; pour water over. Cover the bowl with plastic wrap and let stand for about 12 hours.

Transfer apricots and any liquid to a Dutch oven or large heavy-bottomed pot. Bring to boil over high heat. Reduce heat; cover and simmer for about 15 minutes or until apricots are very soft.

Using a food processor, purée apricots and liquid, in batches, until very smooth. Return purée to the Dutch oven.

Stir in sugar, orange rind, and juice; cook over low heat, stirring constantly, until sugar is dissolved. Increase heat; bring to boil, stirring constantly. Reduce heat; boil gently for 15 to 20 minutes or until thickened. Continue to reduce heat and stir often, especially toward end of cooking time. Test for doneness.

Ladle into sterilized jars to within ¼ inch of rim; wipe rims. Apply prepared lids and rings; tighten just until fingertip tight.

Process jars in boiling water canner for 10 minutes.

Let rest at room temperature until cool. Check seals; refrigerate any unsealed jars for up to three weeks.

Fast Lane

The greater the diameter of the pot, the quicker the fruit butter will thicken as there is a larger area of heat and a greater surface area for evaporation of the liquid.

Blueberry Apple Butter

Use wild blueberries if you can—the flavor is more intense. This butter has a lovely deep-purple color. Try it on pancakes or waffles, or put a little in muffin batter to replace some of the fat.

Prep time: 35 minutes • Cook time: 80 to 95 minutes • Makes about 4 half-pint jars

4 cups wild or cultivated blueberries

8 cups chopped, peeled, and cored apples that soften, about 7 medium apples

1 cup water

3 cups granulated sugar

1 tsp. ground cinnamon

¼ tsp. ground nutmeg

In a Dutch oven or large heavy-bottomed pot, crush blueberries with a potato masher; add apples and water. Bring to boil over high heat. Reduce heat; boil gently for about 20 minutes or until apples are very soft, stirring occasionally.

Purée mixture in food processor until very smooth; return to the clean Dutch oven.

Stir in sugar, cinnamon, and nutmeg; cook over low heat, stirring constantly until sugar is dissolved. Increase heat; bring to boil, stirring constantly. Reduce heat; boil gently for 45 to 60 minutes or until thickened. Continue to reduce heat and stir often, especially toward end of cooking time. Test for doneness.

Fast Lane

To break up the total preparation time, you may do the initial cooking of the fruit and prepare the purée; refrigerate overnight. Then cook it, put into jars and process the next day.

Ladle into sterilized jars to within ¼ inch of rim; wipe rims. Apply prepared lids and rings; tighten just until fingertip tight.

Process jars in boiling water canner for 10 minutes.

Let rest at room temperature until cool. Check seals; refrigerate any unsealed jars for up to three weeks.

Cran-Apple Butter

Two fall favorites partner in this cranberry-red butter. Spread on apple or bran muffins.

Prep time: 45 minutes • Cook time: 45 to 50 minutes • Makes about 5 half-pint jars

2 lb. apples that soften, about 6 medium

3 cups cranberries

2 cups apple cider

2 TB. grated orange peel

3 cups granulated sugar

¼ tsp. ground nutmeg

Cut apples into quarters; remove stems and blossom ends. Slice each quarter into four or five slices. Place apples in a Dutch oven or large heavy-bottomed pot. Stir in cranberries, cider, and orange peel. Bring to boil over high heat. Reduce heat; cover and boil gently for about 15 minutes or until apples are very soft.

Ladle fruit and liquid into a mesh strainer and press pulp through; discard peel and seeds. Or extract pulp using a food mill. Return to the clean Dutch oven.

Stir in sugar and nutmeg; cook over low heat, stirring constantly until sugar is dissolved. Increase heat; bring to boil, stirring constantly. Reduce heat; boil gently, uncovered, for 20 to 25 minutes or until thickened. Continue to reduce heat and stir often, especially toward end of cooking time. Test for doneness.

Ladle into sterilized jars to within ¼ inch of rim; wipe rims. Apply prepared lids and rings; tighten just until fingertip tight.

Process jars in boiling water canner for 10 minutes.

Let rest at room temperature until cool. Check seals; refrigerate any unsealed jars for up to three weeks.

Fruitful Trivia Use frozen cranberries in this recipe, if desired. Measure in a semithawed state while they still hold their shape. If thawed they will squish down and you will have too much.

Mango Butter

Choose fragrant mangoes to make this delicious butter. Whisk some into your favorite vinai-grette for a salad of mixed greens, sliced oranges, and toasted almonds, or into yogurt dressing for fruit salad.

Prep time: 45 minutes • Cook time: 60 to 70 minutes • Makes about 5 half-pint jars

4 lbs. firm, ripe mangoes, about 5 to 6 medium

1⅓ cups apple cider, orange juice, or water

4 cups granulated sugar

2 TB. finely grated lemon rind

⅓ cup lemon juice

Chop mango flesh and place in a Dutch oven or large heavy-bottomed pot. Add cider; bring to boil over high heat. Reduce heat; simmer 15 to 20 minutes until fruit is very soft, stirring occasionally.

Press through a sieve, put through a food mill, or purée in food processor until very smooth; return to the Dutch oven.

Stir in sugar, lemon rind, and juice; cook over low heat, stirring constantly until sugar is dissolved. Increase heat; bring to boil, stirring constantly. Reduce heat; boil gently for 35 to 40 minutes or until thickened. Continue to reduce heat and stir often, especially toward end of cooking time. Test for doneness.

Fruitful Trivia

To check ripeness of mango, press gently with thumb. If it yields slightly to pressure and has a sweet fragrance, then it is ready to use. To hasten ripening, place in paper bag at room temperature. Refrigerate once ripened.

Ladle into sterilized jars to within ¼ inch of rim; wipe rims. Apply prepared lids and rings; tighten just until fingertip tight.

Process jars in boiling water canner for 10 minutes.

Let rest at room temperature until cool. Check seals; refrigerate any unsealed jars for up to three weeks.

Spiced Pear Butter

This caramel-colored butter has a lovely pear flavor and a hint of spice.

Prep time: 40 minutes   •   Cook time: 85 to 100 minutes   •   Makes about 6 half-pint jars

10 lbs. ripe pears

2½ cups apple cider

4½ cups granulated sugar

1 tsp. ground cinnamon

1 tsp. ground ginger

Cut pears into quarters and remove stems and cores (do not peel); coarsely chop. Place in a Dutch oven or large heavy-bottomed pot; stir in cider. Bring to boil over high heat. Reduce heat; cover and boil gently for about 40 minutes or until pears are very soft. After about 30 minutes, use a potato masher to break down pieces further.

Ladle fruit and liquid into a mesh strainer and press pulp through; discard peel. Or extract pulp using a food mill. Return to the clean Dutch oven.

Stir in sugar and spices; cook over low heat, stirring constantly until sugar is dissolved. Increase heat; bring to boil, stirring constantly. Reduce heat; boil gently, uncovered, for 35 to 40 minutes or until thickened. Continue to reduce heat and stir often, especially toward end of cooking time. Test for doneness.

Ladle into sterilized jars to within ¼ inch of rim; wipe rims. Apply prepared lids and rings; tighten just until fingertip tight.

Process jars in boiling water canner for 10 minutes.

Let rest at room temperature until cool. Check seals; refrigerate any unsealed jars for up to three weeks.

Variation

Pear Orange Butter: Substitute orange juice for the apple cider; replace cinnamon and ginger with ½ teaspoon ground nutmeg.

Fruitful Trivia
Pears are intentionally picked while they are underripe (green) and will continue to ripen. Press gently on stem end or shoulders (curve) of the pear. Ripe pears with yield slightly, are fragrant, and begin to turn yellow.

Plum Good Apple Butter

I developed a pie recipe using this combination of fruit and thought I would try it as a butter—it's just as delicious. Excellent on muffins or stirred into plain yogurt.

Prep time: 45 minutes • Cook time: 80 to 90 minutes • Makes about 5 half-pint jars

2 lbs. apples that soften, about 6 medium apples

2 lbs. red plums, pitted and sliced, 16 to 18 medium plums

1½ cups apple cider

3 cups granulated sugar

1 tsp. ground cinnamon

Cut apples into quarters; remove stems and blossom ends. Slice each quarter into four or five slices. Place apples in a Dutch oven or large heavy-bottomed pot; stir in plums and cider. Bring to boil over high heat; reduce heat to medium. Cover; simmer for about 20 minutes or until fruit is very soft.

Ladle fruit and liquid into a mesh strainer and press pulp through; discard peel and seeds. Or extract pulp using a food mill. Return to the clean Dutch oven.

Stir in sugar and cinnamon; cook over low heat, stirring constantly until sugar is dissolved. Increase heat; bring to boil, stirring constantly. Reduce heat; boil gently, uncovered, for 45 to 50 minutes or until thickened. Continue to reduce heat and stir often, especially toward end of cooking time. Test for doneness.

> ### Word to the Wise
> Butters are filled to within ¼ inch of the rim of the jar. This "headspace" is required to create the vacuum for a good, safe seal. They are processed longer than jams though—for 10 minutes.

Ladle into sterilized jars to within ¼ inch of rim; wipe rims. Apply prepared lids and rings; tighten just until fingertip tight.

Process jars in boiling water canner for 10 minutes.

Let rest at room temperature until cool. Check seals; refrigerate any unsealed jars for up to three weeks.

Rhubarb Apple Butter

Once rhubarb gets going, all of a sudden it seems there's too much! Cut it up and freeze to make this fruit butter in the fall for that special flavor you crave.

Prep time: 30 minutes   •   Cook time: 75 to 90 minutes   •   Makes about 4 half-pint jars

4 large apples that soften

6 cups chopped rhubarb

½ cup water

1 large orange, grated rind and juice

5½ cups granulated sugar

Cut apples into quarters; remove stems and blossom ends. Slice each quarter into four or five slices. Place apples in a Dutch oven or large heavy-bottomed pot; stir in rhubarb, water, orange rind, and juice. Bring to boil over high heat; reduce heat to medium. Cover; boil gently for about 15 minutes or until fruit is very soft, stirring occasionally.

Ladle fruit and liquid into a mesh strainer and press pulp through; discard peel and seeds. Or, extract pulp using a food mill. Return to the clean Dutch oven.

Stir in sugar; cook over low heat, stirring constantly, until sugar is dissolved. Increase heat; bring to boil, stirring constantly. Reduce heat; boil gently, uncovered, for 45 to 60 minutes or until thickened. Continue to reduce heat and stir often, especially toward end of cooking time. Test for doneness.

Ladle into sterilized jars to within ¼ inch of rim; wipe rims. Apply prepared lids and rings; tighten just until fingertip tight.

Process jars in boiling water canner for 10 minutes.

Let rest at room temperature until cool. Check seals; refrigerate any unsealed jars for up to three weeks.

Variation

Strawberry Rhubarb Apple Butter: Add a quart of chopped strawberries when cooking and omit orange rind and juice.

Fruitful Trivia
The Strawberry Rhubarb Apple Butter is a good variation use for frozen strawberries, which lose their texture when frozen and then thawed.

The Least You Need to Know

- Fruit butters are great for using up large quantities of fruit, especially apples and pears.
- Apples are a common ingredient of fruit butters and go well in combination with other fruit, giving the butters a pleasing texture.
- Use up apples that are no longer crunchy to make fruit butters.
- Fruit butters do not contain any butter.
- It is important to stir fruit butters often to prevent scorching.
- Fruit butters require 10 minutes of processing. (Don't forget to add more time for higher altitudes.)

Notes

Notes

Chapter 11

Chutneys

In This Chapter

- ◆ What a chutney is
- ◆ Tips for expert ease with chutneys
- ◆ How to test for doneness
- ◆ What to do to prevent and fix errors

Chutneys are a condiment of East Indian origin; they are tangy-sweet, mild-to-hot mixtures of fruit and/or vegetables, sugar, vinegar, and spices, that are cooked until thick, with jamlike consistency. The name comes from *chatni*, which is a Hindi word meaning "strongly spiced."

Chutneys are delicious condiments to serve with curries, hot and cold meats, meat pies, cheese and crackers, and egg dishes, or in wraps. Stir some into stuffing mixtures for poultry or pork-loin roast. They have the sweetness and consistency of a jam and contain fruit, but border on a relish with their savory hot-and-spicy ingredients.

The flavor of a chutney improves with age; most are best after resting for at least one month. Chutneys are slowly simmered to reach a thick consistency, so they do not require added pectin. They are like jam, but the consistency is soft and spoonable. Also, the pieces of fruit tend to be larger, as in a conserve.

The flavor is a balance of sweetness from the fruit and sugar with acid from vinegar, citrus juice, or apple cider. Herbs have been used in some of the recipes to enhance flavor. I have made use of a variety of dried fruit for color, flavor, and texture. You can vary the type of vinegar in the recipes, choosing from white, malt, apple cider, red or white wine, and so on. Most vinegars are 5 percent acetic acid (check the packaging). You may replace some of the white sugar with brown for a deeper color and flavor.

Hotness can be adjusted to suit your own taste. Turn up the heat with fresh chili peppers, such as jalapeños, red finger chilis, habañeros, hot (crushed) red chili-pepper flakes, cayenne pepper, or hot pepper sauce.

Word to the Wise

Please review Chapter 1 to reacquaint yourself with preserve-making. Things may have changed since you first started making preserves. If you are a beginner, there are a few important things to know before getting started. Many instructions are common to all preserves so, once you get it right for one, you'll sail through the others. It's a lot easier than you might think.

Tips for Prizewinning Chutneys

Stop here before beginning to cook for tips on how to get expert results:

◆ Choose top-quality, firm, ripe fruit. Trim any bad spots or blemishes; chop coarsely or slice in larger pieces than you would for jams.

◆ Ensure that spices are fresh; smell to see if aroma is strong. Adjust heat level according to taste.

◆ For chutneys, usually all the ingredients except the dried fruit are stirred together and cooked down, uncovered. Dried fruit is often added halfway through, or near the end of cooking, to prevent it from sinking to the bottom and scorching.

◆ Stir often to prevent mixture from scorching, especially as the chutney thickens; reduce heat as it thickens, but keep it gently bubbling. Place a wire star underneath the pot, if desired, to even out heat and prevent hot spots. The secret is the long, slow cooking. The greater the diameter of the pot, the more evenly chutney will cook.

- Begin to test for doneness (see details following) when chutney starts to thicken.
- Fill jars to within ½ inch of jar rim; process for 10 minutes. Slide a nonmetal tool such as rubber scraper between the jar and the chutney, to remove air pockets.

Test for Doneness

Place a spoonful of chutney on a plate. Draw a small spoon through the center. Chutney tests done when no liquid seeps into the space. Chutney will thicken more as it cools and should not be overly thick. It should mound on a spoon but fall gently from it.

Word to the Wise

Read through the entire recipe before beginning, even if you have made it before. Make sure to add ingredients in the order given.

Word to the Wise

I define the cook time at the beginning of each recipe as the overall "estimated" cooking time to heat and bring mixtures to a boil as well as the boiling or simmering time specified in the recipe. With preserving (vs. other regular cooking recipes) the time will vary with the type of pot used (metal, glass, size) and how often it is stirred, etc.

Troubleshooting Tips and Quick Fixes

In this section you will find practical tips and information on how to fix or prevent some of the common chutney-making errors. A quick read through them may help save problems later.

Problem: Chutney shrinks in the jar.

It's likely chutney was overcooked or stored in too warm a place. Store in a cool, dark, dry place.

Problem: Liquid on the surface.

The chutney was not cooked long enough to evaporate liquid. Ensure complete cooking by testing for doneness.

Apple Chutney

This is a great chutney to make during apple harvest. It is especially delicious with roast pork or in a pork or chicken sandwich.

Prep time: 55 minutes • Cook time: 40 to 45 minutes • Makes about 5 half-pint jars

4 cups chopped, peeled apples that keep their shape

4 cups chopped, peeled apples that soften

2 cups chopped onion

2 cups apple cider

1½ cups packed brown sugar

1 cup cider vinegar

⅔ cup seedless golden raisins

2 cloves garlic, minced

2 TB. grated fresh ginger

1 tsp. salt

¾ tsp. ground cinnamon

½ tsp. ground coriander

½ tsp. hot red chili-pepper flakes

In a Dutch oven or large heavy-bottomed pot, mix together apples, onion, apple cider, brown sugar, raisins, garlic, ginger, salt, cinnamon, coriander, and red chili-pepper flakes. Bring to boil over high heat, stirring often.

Word to the Wise

Stir chutney often to prevent scorching, especially as the mixture thickens; reduce heat as it thickens, but keep it gently bubbling. Place a wire star underneath the pot, if desired, to even out heat and prevent hot spots.

Reduce heat; boil gently for 30 to 35 minutes or until thickened, stirring often. Reduce heat further and stir more often as it thickens. Test for doneness.

Ladle into sterilized jars to within ½ inch of rim; wipe rims. Apply prepared lids and rings; tighten rings just until fingertip tight.

Process jars in boiling water canner for 10 minutes.

Let rest at room temperature until cooled. Check seals; refrigerate any unsealed jars for up to three weeks.

Golden Apple Plum Chutney

In this chutney, golden apples are paired with yellow plums and golden raisins. There are no chilis in this recipe, but feel free to add some.

Prep time: 50 minutes   •   Cook time: 50 to 55 minutes   •   Makes about 6 half-pint jars

4 large Golden Delicious apples, peeled, cored, and chopped, about 2 lbs.

4½ cups thinly sliced yellow plums, about 1½ lbs.

2½ cups granulated sugar

2 cups chopped onion

1 cup seedless golden raisins

1 cup cider vinegar

1 tsp. salt

¼ tsp. ground cloves

In a Dutch oven or large heavy-bottomed pot, mix together apples, plums, sugar, onion, raisins, vinegar, salt, and cloves. Bring to boil over high heat, stirring often.

Reduce heat; boil gently for 40 to 45 minutes or until thickened, stirring often. Reduce heat further and stir more often as it thickens. Test for doneness.

Word to the Wise

Cloves can be an overpowering spice, so measure carefully. Always check the freshness of your spices by smelling. If they smell only moderately fragrant, it is likely time to buy fresh ones.

Ladle into sterilized jars to within ½ inch of rim; wipe rims. Apply prepared lids and rings; tighten rings just until fingertip tight.

Process jars in boiling water canner for 10 minutes.

Let rest at room temperature until cooled. Check seals; refrigerate any unsealed jars for up to three weeks.

Apricot Chutney

Try this tasty chutney in your next chicken or turkey sandwich or wrap.

Prep time: 40 minutes • Cook time: 55 to 65 minutes • Makes about 7 half-pint jars

5 cups dried apricots

4 cups boiling water

2¾ cups granulated sugar

1½ cups chopped onion, optional

1¼ cups vinegar

2 TB. finely grated fresh ginger

1 TB. crushed or puréed garlic

½ tsp. cayenne pepper, or hot red chili-pepper flakes

¼ tsp. pickling or regular salt

1 cup golden seedless raisins

In a large bowl, combine apricots and boiling water. Cover; let stand for eight hours or overnight. Cut each apricot into 4 slices.

In a Dutch oven or large heavy-bottomed pot, mix together apricots plus liquid and sugar, onion (if using), vinegar, ginger, garlic, cayenne pepper, and salt. Bring to boil over high heat, stirring often.

Reduce heat; boil gently for about 45 minutes, stirring often. Stir in raisins and cook for about 10 minutes longer or until thickened, stirring often. Reduce heat further and stir more often as it thickens. Test for doneness.

Fruitful Trivia

Dried fruit is often added halfway through, or near the end of cooking, to prevent it from sinking to the bottom and scorching.

Ladle into sterilized jars to within ½ inch of rim; wipe rims. Apply prepared lids and rings; tighten rings just until fingertip tight.

Process jars in boiling water canner for 10 minutes.

Let rest at room temperature until cooled. Check seals; refrigerate any unsealed jars for up to three weeks.

Cran-Apple Sage and Thyme Chutney

This is the kind of chutney you'll want to eat with roasted turkey, chicken, or pork, or to add to your stuffing. The flavor of herbs is a nice variation on traditional chutneys, which are primarily seasoned with spices and hot peppers.

Prep time: 45 minutes • Cook time: 55 to 65 minutes • Makes about 4 half-pint jars

1 TB. oil

1½ cups chopped onion

2 cloves garlic, minced

3 cups chopped, peeled apples that keep their shape

3 cups chopped, peeled apples that soften

3 cups fresh or frozen cranberries

2½ cups granulated sugar

2 cups water

1 cup cider vinegar

1 tsp. salt

1 tsp. dried sage

¾ tsp. dried thyme

In a Dutch oven or large heavy-bottomed pot over medium-high heat, heat oil. Add onions; cook for about seven minutes or until softened. Add garlic; cook for two minutes.

Add apples, cranberries, sugar, water, vinegar, salt, sage, and thyme. Bring to boil over high heat, stirring often. Reduce heat; boil gently for 35 to 40 minutes or until thickened, stirring often. Reduce heat further and stir more often as it thickens. Test for doneness.

Ladle into sterilized jars to within ½ inch of rim; wipe rims. Apply prepared lids and rings; tighten rings just until fingertip tight.

Process jars in boiling water canner for 10 minutes.

Let rest at room temperature until cooled. Check seals; refrigerate any unsealed jars for up to three weeks.

Word to the Wise
The secret to great chutney is the long, slow cooking. The greater the diameter of the pot, the more evenly it will cook.

Date Orange Chutney

This chutney has a lovely orange-red color and subtle orange flavor. It is not too sweet and has just a touch of heat, which you may increase if you like. Serve with aged cheddar cheese on crackers, or with chicken, pork, or scrambled eggs.

Prep time: 45 minutes • Cook time: 60 to 65 minutes • Makes about 5 half-pint jars

2 cups chopped dates, about 1 lb.

2 cups chopped, peeled oranges, about 4 large oranges

3¾ cups packed brown sugar

2¾ cups white wine vinegar

2 cups chopped onion

1 cup seedless golden raisins

2 TB. finely grated orange rind

1 TB. minced fresh ginger

1½ tsp. ground coriander

1 tsp. salt

¼ tsp. hot red chili-pepper flakes

In a Dutch oven or large heavy-bottomed pot, mix together dates, oranges, brown sugar, vinegar, onion, raisins, orange rind, ginger, coriander, salt, and chili-pepper flakes. Bring to boil over high heat, stirring often.

Word to the Wise

Preserves are sealed when lids curve inward. Test seal by pressing down in the center—if the lid moves, then it has not sealed, so refrigerate immediately. For stored preserves, discard anywhere the lids have popped up.

Reduce heat; boil gently for 55 to 60 minutes or until thickened, stirring often. Reduce heat further and stir more often as it thickens. Test for doneness.

Ladle into sterilized jars to within ½ inch of rim; wipe rims. Apply prepared lids and rings; tighten rings just until fingertip tight.

Process jars in boiling water canner for 10 minutes.

Let rest at room temperature until cooled. Check seals; refrigerate any unsealed jars for up to three weeks.

Green Tomato Apple Chutney

Make this sensational chutney in early September, when the last of the tomatoes are struggling to ripen and the new harvest of apples appears in the stores. Serve with scrambled eggs, quiche, and omelets. Stir into hash-brown potatoes or serve with cheese or cold meat.

Prep time: 60 minutes • Cook time: 65 to 70 minutes • Makes about 6 half-pint jars

7 cups chopped green or partially ripe tomatoes cut into ½-inch chunks, about 3 lbs.

4 cups peeled apples that soften, cut into
½-inch chunks

1½ cups chopped onion

1½ cups packed brown sugar

1 cup granulated sugar

1 cup cider vinegar

1 large clove garlic, minced

2 TB. whole mustard seed

2 TB. finely grated fresh ginger

1 tsp. salt

½ tsp. hot red chili-pepper flakes or cayenne
pepper

¼ tsp. ground cloves

1 cup sultana raisins

In a Dutch oven or large heavy-bottomed pot, mix together tomatoes, apples, onion, brown sugar, granulated sugar, vinegar, garlic, mustard seed, ginger, salt, chili-pepper flakes, and cloves. Bring to boil over high heat, stirring often.

Reduce heat; boil gently for 40 to 50 minutes, stirring often. Stir in raisins and cook for about 15 minutes longer or until thickened, stirring often. Reduce heat further and stir more often as it thickens. Test for doneness.

Word to the Wise

Chutneys are filled to within ½ inch of the rim of the jar (headspace). Leaving this exact space is important for creating the vacuum for a good, safe seal. If filled too full, contents may see through lid while processing and interfere with the seal.

Ladle into sterilized jars to within ½ inch of rim; wipe rims. Apply prepared lids and rings; tighten rings just until fingertip tight.

Process jars in boiling water canner for 10 minutes.

Let rest at room temperature until cooled. Check seals; refrigerate any unsealed jars for up to three weeks.

Mango Chutney

Mango chutney is perhaps the most popular chutney, easily found in supermarkets and gourmet stores. It is the perfect accompaniment to East Indian dishes, providing sweet, tart, and hot tastes. Also nice served with cheese on crackers.

Prep time: 50 minutes • Cook time: 75 to 85 minutes • Makes about 4 half-pint jars

1 TB. oil

2 cups chopped onions

3 cloves garlic, minced

¼ cup diced red bell pepper

2 TB. grated fresh ginger

1 TB. minced red or green hot chili pepper

6 cups chopped mangoes, about 4½ lbs. or 5 medium mangoes

2½ cups packed brown sugar

1 cup cider vinegar

1 TB. lime juice

½ tsp. salt

¼ tsp. ground allspice

6 whole cloves

In a Dutch oven or large heavy-bottomed pot over medium heat, heat oil. Add onions; cook for about seven minutes or until softened.

Stir in garlic, sweet red pepper, ginger, and hot pepper; cook, stirring, for two minutes.

Stir in mangoes, brown sugar, vinegar, lime juice, salt, allspice, and cloves. Bring to boil over high heat, stirring often.

Reduce heat; boil gently for 50 to 60 minutes or until thickened, stirring often. Reduce heat further and stir more often as it thickens. Test for doneness.

Ladle into sterilized jars to within ½ inch of rim; wipe rims. Apply prepared lids and rings; tighten rings just until fingertip tight.

Process jars in boiling water canner for 10 minutes.

Let rest at room temperature until cool. Check seals; refrigerate any unsealed jars for up to three weeks.

Fast Lane

Use a magnetic wand (a plastic wand with a magnet attached to the end) to quickly lift prepared jar lids from hot water. Look for them with the canning tools in kitchen supplies or hardware stores.

Mango Peach Chutney

Mango and peach create a powerful combination in this hot and spicy chutney. Excellent served with East Indian dishes, pork chops, or roast chicken. Use to top Baked Brie.

Prep time: 55 minutes • Cook time: 65 to 90 minutes • Makes about 6 half-pint jars

4 cups chopped mangoes, about 3 lbs. or 3 to
4 medium mangoes

4 cups chopped, peeled peaches

1 large onion, diced

1 red bell pepper, diced

2 large cloves garlic, minced

1½ cups packed brown sugar

1 cup cider vinegar

½ cup seedless golden raisins

¼ cup lime juice

1 tsp. salt

1 tsp. ground allspice

1 tsp. ground cinnamon

½ tsp. ground ginger

½ tsp. turmeric

⅛ to ¼ tsp. cayenne pepper, or 1 or 2 jalapeño
peppers, finely chopped

In a Dutch oven or large heavy-bottomed pot, mix together mangoes, peaches, onion, pepper, garlic, brown sugar, vinegar, raisins, lime juice, salt, allspice, cinnamon, ginger, turmeric, and pepper. Bring to boil over high heat, stirring often.

Reduce heat; boil gently for one to one and a half hours or until thickened, stirring often. Reduce heat further and stir more often as it thickens. Test for doneness.

Word to the Wise

Chutneys are processed in a boiling water canner for 10 minutes. This amount of time is required as chutneys are not as high in sugar as jams and other sweeter preserves.

Ladle into sterilized jars to within ½ inch of rim; wipe rims. Apply prepared lids and rings; tighten rings just until fingertip tight.

Process jars in boiling water canner for 10 minutes.

Let rest at room temperature until cooled. Check seals; refrigerate any unsealed jars for up to three weeks.

Variation

Mango Nectarine Chutney: Substitute unpeeled nectarines for the peaches.

Peach Plum Chutney

Try making this chutney in late August when both of these fruits are in season. Serve with poultry or pork.

Prep time: 60 minutes   •   Cook time: 55 to 70 minutes   •   Makes about 5 half-pint jars

3 cups chopped, peeled, and pitted, peaches, about 1½ lbs.

4 cups chopped, and pitted yellow or red plums, about 1½ lbs.

2½ cups packed brown sugar

1 cup diced yellow or red bell pepper

1 cup chopped onion

1 large clove garlic, minced

1 green or red chili pepper, minced, or 1 tsp. hot red chili-pepper flakes

⅔ cup white wine vinegar

2 TB. finely grated fresh ginger

1 TB. finely grated lemon rind

2 tsp. salt

1 tsp. ground cinnamon

1 tsp. ground cloves

1 tsp. whole mustard seed

½ tsp. ground coriander

½ tsp. turmeric

In a Dutch oven or large heavy-bottomed pot, mix together peaches, plums, brown sugar, bell pepper, onion, garlic, chili-pepper, vinegar, ginger, lemon rind, salt, cinnamon, cloves, mustard seed, coriander, and turmeric. Bring to boil over high heat, stirring often.

Reduce heat; boil gently for 45 to 60 minutes or until thickened, stirring often. Reduce heat further and stir more often as it thickens. Test for doneness.

Ladle into sterilized jars to within ½ inch of rim; wipe rims. Apply prepared lids and rings; tighten rings just until fingertip tight.

Process jars in boiling water canner for 10 minutes.

Let rest at room temperature until cooled. Check seals; refrigerate any unsealed jars for up to three weeks.

Variation

Nectarine Plum Chutney: Substitute unpeeled nectarines for the peaches.

Fruitful Trivia _____

Fresh ginger, also known as gingerroot is a knobby root with a thin tan-colored skin that is removed before using. It has a slightly sweet, peppery flavor with a touch of hotness. Avoid ginger with wrinkled skin. Store unpeeled ginger, tightly wrapped in plastic, in refrigerator up to three weeks or freeze up to six months.

Pear Cranberry Chutney

This is another lovely fall chutney, perfect for eating with roast turkey or chicken, or to stir into stuffing. It leans toward the savory, with the inclusion of thyme and exclusion of hot peppers.

Prep time: 30 minutes • Cook time: 55 to 70 minutes • Makes about 5 half-pint jars

5 cups chopped, peeled, and cored pears,
about 4 lbs. or 5 large pears

3 cups fresh or frozen cranberries

3 cups granulated sugar

1½ cups chopped onion

1 cup red wine vinegar

1 TB. ground ginger

½ tsp. dried thyme, or 1 tsp. finely chopped
fresh thyme

In a Dutch oven or large heavy-bottomed pot, mix together pears, cranberries, sugar, onion, vinegar, ginger, and thyme. Bring to boil over high heat, stirring often.

Reduce heat; boil gently for 45 to 60 minutes or until thickened, stirring often. Reduce heat further and stir more often as it thickens. Test for doneness.

Fruitful Trivia _____
To remove fresh thyme leaves from their stems, pull gently down the stem against the direction of growth and they will come off a lot more easily. For a flavor variation, try using fresh lemon thyme (which is easy to grow).

Ladle into sterilized jars to within ½ inch of rim; wipe rims. Apply prepared lids and rings; tighten rings just until fingertip tight.

Process jars in boiling water canner for 10 minutes.

Let rest at room temperature until cooled. Check seals; refrigerate any unsealed jars for up to three weeks.

Pineapple Chutney

This colorful chutney goes well with ham, roast pork, pork chops, or chicken. Stir into plain yogurt for an interesting dip for veggies or chicken wings.

Prep time: 50 minutes • Cook time: 50 to 60 minutes • Makes about 4 half-pint jars

4 cups chopped fresh pineapple, about 1 medium pineapple

2 large apples that soften, peeled and diced

1½ cups chopped red onion

1 TB. grated fresh ginger, or ½ tsp. ground ginger

⅓ cup each chopped red and green bell pepper

1 TB. minced hot pepper, such as jalapeño

1¾ cups packed brown sugar

1 cup cider vinegar

⅓ cup sultana raisins

½ tsp. ground cloves

Pinch salt

In a Dutch oven or large heavy-bottomed pot, mix together pineapple, apples, onion, ginger, bell peppers, hot pepper, brown sugar, vinegar, raisins, cloves, and salt. Bring to boil over high heat, stirring often.

Word to the Wise

Use caution when handling hot (chili) peppers. Use plastic gloves and avoid touching your eyes. The membranes and seeds account for 80 percent of the capsaicin, which gives the peppers their fire. Change the type of chili to suit your personal taste and tolerance!

Reduce heat; boil gently for 40 to 50 minutes or until thickened, stirring often. Reduce heat further and stir more often as it thickens. Test for doneness.

Ladle into sterilized jars to within ½ inch of rim; wipe rims. Apply prepared lids and rings; tighten rings just until fingertip tight.

Process jars in boiling water canner for 10 minutes.

Let rest at room temperature until cooled. Check seals; refrigerate any unsealed jars for up to three weeks.

Plum Pear Chutney

In this chutney, pieces of pear are surrounded by a dark, savory mixture. Serve with pork roast or chops; stir into sauce for pork tenderloin.

Prep time: 50 minutes   •   Cook time: 55 to 70 minutes   •   Makes about 5 half-pint jars

4 cups pitted, sliced red plums, about 1½ lbs.
(about 6 large plums)

3 cups chopped, peeled, and cored Bartlett
pears (4 to 5 large pears)

1 large apple (any type), peeled and sliced

3½ cups packed brown sugar

1½ cups chopped onion

1½ cups cider vinegar

½ cup dried cranberries

½ tsp. ground nutmeg (optional)

In a Dutch oven or large heavy-bottomed pot, mix together plums, pears, apple, brown sugar, onion, vinegar, cranberries, and nutmeg (if using). Bring to boil over high heat, stirring often.

Reduce heat; boil gently for 45 to 60 minutes or until thickened, stirring often. Reduce heat further and stir more often as it thickens. Test for doneness.

Ladle into sterilized jars to within ½ inch of rim; wipe rims. Apply prepared lids and rings; tighten rings just until fingertip tight.

Process jars in boiling water canner for 10 minutes.

Let rest at room temperature until cooled. Check seals; refrigerate any unsealed jars for up to three weeks.

Fruitful Trivia

If desired, use dried sour cherries in place of dried cranberries, as their tart flavor also works well with the pear and plum flavors.

Sweet-Pepper Apple Chutney

This is a beautiful-looking chutney, containing red bell peppers and dried currants. For a different taste, substitute roasted red bell peppers for the fresh ones. Excellent served with poultry or pork.

Prep time: 45 minutes • Cook time: 55 to 60 minutes • Makes about 5 half-pint jars

5 cups chopped, peeled apples that hold their shape, about 2 lbs. or 5 medium apples

2 cups chopped red bell pepper

2 cups packed brown sugar

1½ cups chopped onion

1 cup chopped yellow bell pepper

2 or 3 cloves garlic, minced

1 cup cider vinegar

1 tsp. salt

½ tsp. ground cloves

½ tsp. hot red chili-pepper flakes

¼ tsp. pepper

½ cup dried currants

In a Dutch oven or large heavy-bottomed pot, mix together apples, red bell pepper, brown sugar, onion, yellow bell pepper, garlic, vinegar, salt, cloves, chili-pepper flakes, and pepper. Bring to boil over high heat, stirring often.

Word to the Wise

For best taste, allow chutneys to rest for at least a month before opening to allow their flavors to fully develop and blend.

Reduce heat; boil gently for about 30 minutes, stirring often. Stir in currants; cook for 15 minutes longer or until thickened, stirring often. Reduce heat further and stir more often as it thickens. Test for doneness.

Ladle into sterilized jars to within ½ inch of rim; wipe rims. Apply prepared lids and rings; tighten rings just until fingertip tight.

Process jars in boiling water canner for 10 minutes.

Let rest at room temperature until cooled. Check seals; refrigerate any unsealed jars for up to three weeks.

Variation

Sweet-Pepper Peach Chutney: Substitute chopped, peeled peaches for the apples.

The Least You Need to Know

- Long, slow cooking in a wide diameter pot is the secret to great chutney.
- Make chutneys as hot or as mild as you like by adjusting the amount and type of hot peppers added.
- Chutneys require a ½ inch headspace and 10 minutes of processing time.
- Chutneys taste best after resting for a month.

Notes

Notes

12

Recipes Using Preserves

In This Chapter

- ◆ Recipes to enjoy homemade preserves on
- ◆ Desserts that use preserves as ingredients

In this chapter, you will find some tasty recipes with preserves as the secret ingredient! Preserves make great ingredients and add a lot of flavor and interest to desserts. They add a touch of sweetness and fruit flavor, whether as a glaze for a fruit tart, to enhance French toast, as a fill for fancy braided bread, a flavoring for cookies and cakes, or a sauce for fried bananas. Use your imagination to jazz up your own sweet recipes, too.

Cream Tea Scones

My favorite way to enjoy preserves is on fresh-baked scones. The recipe for these light, delicious scones comes from Carol Ferguson, former food editor of *Canadian Living* and *Homemaker's* magazines, and author of the recently published *The New Canadian Basics Cookbook* (Penguin, 1999).

Prep time: 20 minutes • Cook time: 10 to 12 minutes • Makes about 10 scones

2 cups all-purpose flour, or 1 cup each
all-purpose and cake and pastry flours

2 TB. granulated sugar

1 TB. baking powder

½ tsp. salt

½ cup butter, softened

1 egg

⅔ cup milk or light cream

In a large bowl, mix together flour, sugar, baking powder, and salt.

Using a pastry blender, cut in butter until mixture resembles coarse crumbs.

In a small bowl, beat egg; reserve 1 tablespoon to brush on top of scones before baking. Stir together remaining egg and milk.

Using a fork, stir egg mixture into flour mixture to make a light, soft dough. If dough seems too sticky, stir in a bit more flour.

Gather dough into a ball; knead lightly a few times on a lightly floured surface until smooth. Flatten with hands or rolling pin to ¾-inch thickness. Cut into 2½-inch rounds; place on ungreased baking sheet. Brush tops with reserved egg. Sprinkle tops with a little sugar, if desired.

Word to the Wise
For light, flaky scones that are not tough, don't handle the dough any more than you have to.

Bake in a preheated 425°F oven for 10 to 12 minutes or until golden brown. Reduce oven temperature if scones begin to brown too quickly; your oven may be hotter than it says. Serve hot.

Variation

For wedges, divide dough into two rounds; lightly dust top of each with flour and place on a baking sheet. With floured knife, cut each round into six wedges but do not separate. Brush tops with reserved egg; sprinkle with sugar. Bake about 15 minutes or until golden brown. Makes 12 wedges.

Stuffed French Toast

This is a recipe I developed for the Ontario Egg Producers. It's a special version of French toast with a delightful surprise filling. Use jams made from strawberry, peach, cherry, blueberry, apricot, and so on.

Prep time: 25 minutes • Cook time: 12 to 15 minutes • Makes 4 servings

8 slices French *baguette*, diagonally cut in
1½-inch slices

½ cup cream cheese, softened

1 TB. jam (strawberry jam, blueberry banana
jam, or cherry raspberry jam)

4 eggs

½ cup milk

½ tsp. vanilla

2 TB. oil

Open bread by cutting a slit into each slice—cut each piece as if you are making two slices each ¾-inch thick, but do not cut all the way through.

Well Defined

A **baguette** is a long, thin French-style bread, sometimes known as French stick bread. For this recipe look for one with a diameter of about three to four-inches. You may also use eight slices of egg bread to make this recipes.

Mix together cream cheese and jam; spread about 1 tablespoon filling evenly into each slit. Press gently to close.

In a medium bowl, whisk together eggs, milk, and vanilla. Dip each stuffed bread slice into egg mixture to coat on both sides. If bread is dry, leave longer to soak.

In a nonstick skillet over medium heat, heat 1 tablespoon oil. Cook half of stuffed bread until golden brown on each side, one to two minutes per side. Repeat with remaining bread, adding more oil as needed. Serve drizzled with warmed jam or maple syrup and whipped cream, if desired.

Easy Coffee Cake

This cake takes just a few minutes to stir together. Use any of your jams or conserves to give it a special flavor. The nuts will toast as it bakes.

Prep time: 20 minutes • Cook time: 30 to 35 minutes • Makes about 8 servings

1½ cups all-purpose flour

½ cup granulated sugar

2 tsp. baking powder

½ tsp. salt

1 egg

¾ cup milk

½ cup vegetable oil

½ tsp. vanilla

¼ cup jam (any kind)

2 TB. sliced almonds, or chopped pecans or walnuts (optional)

In a large bowl, mix together flour, sugar, baking powder, and salt.

In a separate bowl, whisk together egg, milk, oil, and vanilla. Stir egg mixture into flour until just combined.

Spoon batter into a greased eight-inch square cake pan. Dot with jam and sprinkle with nuts, if using.

Bake in a preheated 350°F oven for about 30 minutes or until golden and tester inserted in center comes out clean. Serve warm.

![Fast Lane icon] **Fast Lane**

To save time, you can prepare parts of this recipe ahead. Measure and stir together dry ingredients; cover and set aside. Measure egg, milk, oil, and vanilla together; cover and refrigerate. Assembly is now quick and you will have a lovely cake to serve hot out of the oven.

Fruit Loaf

Make this loaf with the following marmalades: lemon ginger, lemon lime; cranberry, peach, carrot or zucchini orange; pineapple citrus; or three-fruit. Chop peel smaller if marmalade has large pieces. After cooling, wrap the loaf well and cut the next day. It freezes well, too.

Prep time: 20 minutes • Cook time: 50 to 60 minutes • Makes 1 loaf

½ cup butter, softened

½ cup granulated sugar

2 eggs

½ tsp. vanilla

¾ cup marmalade

2 cups all-purpose flour

1½ tsp. baking powder

½ tsp. salt

⅔ cup milk

Glaze (optional):

¼ cup lemon or lime juice

¼ cup granulated sugar

In a large bowl, using an electric mixer, cream together butter, sugar, eggs, and vanilla; beat in marmalade.

In a separate bowl, mix together flour, baking powder, and salt; stir into creamed mixture alternately with milk.

Pour into a greased and floured 9×5-inch loaf pan. Bake in preheated 350°F oven for 50 to 60 minutes or until tester inserted in center comes out clean. (Reduce oven temperature to 325°F for glass or dark baking pans and bake a little longer.) Let cool in pan for 10 minutes; then turn out onto rack to cool.

 Word to the Wise

Be sure to keep baking powder tightly sealed at all times. To see if it is still effective, mix a teaspoon of it into ⅓ cup water. If it is very bubbly, it is fine.

Glaze, if desired, while still warm. In a small bowl, mix together lemon juice and sugar. Prick the surface of cake with toothpick or skewer; slowly pour glaze over loaf, letting it soak in.

Variation

Lemon Ginger Poppyseed Loaf: Add 2 tablespoons poppyseeds to flour mixture.

Empire Cookies

These are a sandwich-style cookies filled with jam. Try apricot, blackberry, boysenberry, cherry, plum, or strawberry jams instead of raspberry. Press jams with large pieces through a sieve before spreading on cookies. Use cookie cutters with scalloped edges if you can. This recipe is from Pat Moynihan-Morris, who makes them for courses she teaches on teas.

Prep time: 25 minutes   •   Cook time: 8 to 10 minutes   •   Makes about 2 dozen

½ cup butter, softened

¼ cup shortening, softened

¾ cup granulated sugar

2 eggs

1 tsp. vanilla

2¼ cups all-purpose flour

1 ½ tsp. baking powder

¼ tsp. salt

½ cup Raspberry Jam

Icing:

1½ cups sifted *icing sugar*

¼ tsp. almond extract

2 TB. (approx.) hot water

Candied cherries to decorate (optional)

In a large bowl, using an electric mixer, cream together butter, shortening, sugar, eggs, and vanilla.

In a separate bowl, mix together flour, baking powder, and salt; stir into creamed mixture. Form dough into ball and chill for one hour.

On lightly floured surface, roll out dough to ¼-inch thickness. Cut into two-inch rounds; place on ungreased baking sheets.

Bake in a preheated 350°F oven for 8 to 10 minutes or until lightly browned around edges. Remove to cooling racks; let cool completely.

Spread half of the cookies with jam.

Combine icing sugar, almond extract, and enough of the hot water to make a thin icing. Frost remaining cookies; decorate each with small piece of candied cherry, if desired. Place tops on jam filling.

Variation

Valentine Cookies: Cut cookies with a heart-shape cookie cutter. If desired, use a smaller heart cutter to cut holes in top half of cookies. Bake cut-out pieces, too, and make little heart cookies.

Well Defined

Icing sugar is also known as confectioners' or powdered sugar. It is granulated sugar that has been crushed into a powder. A bit of cornstarch is added to prevent clumping. Its quick-dissolving ability makes it ideal for icings. If desired, sprinkle icing sugar directly onto the top of cakes or cookies by spooning into a fine sieve and shaking over top.

Marmalade Pecan Cookies

These soft cookies with a nutty crunch can be made with the following marmalades: lemon ginger; carrot, peach, or zucchini orange; or three-fruit.

Prep time: 25 minutes • Cook time: 10 to 12 minutes • Makes 2 to 3 dozen

½ cup butter, softened

½ cup packed brown sugar

1 egg

½ tsp. vanilla

½ cup marmalade or conserve

2¼ cups all-purpose flour

2 tsp. baking powder

½ tsp. ground cinnamon

¼ tsp. baking soda

¼ tsp. salt

¾ cup coarsely chopped pecans or walnuts
(optional)

In a large bowl, with an electric mixer, cream together butter, sugar, egg, and vanilla; beat in marmalade.

In a separate bowl, mix together flour, baking powder, cinnamon, baking soda, and salt; stir into creamed mixture just until combined. Stir in pecans, if using.

Drop spoonfuls onto greased baking sheets. Bake in a preheated 350°F oven for 10 to 12 minutes or until lightly browned.

Variations

Caribbean Treasure Cookies: Use Caribbean Treasure conserve; add ½ cup shredded coconut with the pecans. Or use carrot apple mincemeat in place of marmalade and omit cinnamon and pecans.

Word to the Wise

Don't use butter for greasing baking sheets—it can burn. Use vegetable shortening or a baking spray for best results.

French Apple Tarts

I developed this recipe for the Ontario Apple Producers. Apricot jam mixed with brandy is used to glaze fruit after tarts are baked. Using frozen puff pastry makes it easy to prepare this elegant dessert.

Prep time: 25 minutes • Cook time: 25 to 30 minutes • Makes 8 tarts

1 (approximately 17.3 oz) pkg. frozen puff pastry, thawed

4 large apples that hold their shape, peeled, cored, and sliced

1 TB. lemon juice

2 TB. granulated sugar

½ tsp. ground cinnamon

¼ cup apricot jam, orange marmalade, or red currant jelly

2 tsp. apricot brandy or orange liqueur

On a lightly floured surface, roll out half of the puff pastry into a nine-inch square. Cut into four 4½-inch squares; place on a baking sheet. Repeat with remaining pastry.

In a large bowl, toss apple slices with lemon juice. In a small bowl, mix together 1 tablespoon sugar and the cinnamon; stir into apples.

Word to the Wise

To prevent errors, always read a recipe through before beginning preparation and pre-heat the oven.

Arrange apple slices on pastry, overlapping slightly. Bake in a preheated 400°F oven for 15 minutes; sprinkle remaining 1 tablespoon sugar over apples. Return to oven; bake for about 10 minutes longer or until pastry is puffed and golden.

In a small bowl, mix together jam and brandy; brush over warm tarts to glaze. Serve warm or at room temperature.

Pineapple Tartlets

This recipe is from my friend Pat Moynihan-Morris's Auntie Ev, who makes them every Christmas. They quickly disappear from her cookie tray. They would be good with any jam.

Prep time: 30 minutes   •   Cook time: 8 to 10 minutes   •   Makes about 2 dozen mini tarts.

1 cup butter, softened

2 TB. granulated sugar

1 egg

2 TB. milk

1 tsp. vanilla

2 cups all-purpose flour

4 tsp. baking powder

¼ tsp. salt

⅓ cup piña colada jam (approximate) or pineapple citrus marmalade

In a large bowl, using an electric mixer, cream together butter and sugar. Beat in egg, milk, and vanilla.

In a separate bowl, mix together flour, baking powder, and salt; stir into creamed mixture.

On a lightly floured surface, roll out dough to ¼-inch thickness. Cut into two-inch squares; fit into mini-tart tins.

Place about 1 teaspoon jam into each tart; fold four corners of pastry over jam.

Bake in a preheated 400°F oven for 8 to 10 minutes or until lightly browned.

Word to the Wise

A good oven thermometer is a great investment—many ovens are hotter or cooler than they should be! Always check for doneness at the earliest time indicated (if recipe says to bake for 8 to 10 minutes, check first at 8 minutes).

Lime Phyllo Tarts or Pie

Spoon filling into light, crispy phyllo cups and garnish with dollop of whipped cream, raspberries, and a mint sprig. Or spoon into prepared pie shell, top with whipped cream, and garnish with small slices of fresh lime.

Prep time: 20 minutes; add 20 minutes if making phyllo cups or preparing crumb crust   •
Cook time: 6 to 8 minutes for phyllo cups   •   Makes 8 pie servings or 9 phyllo cups

1 (250 g) pkg. cream cheese, softened

½ cup lime or lemon-lime marmalade

4 TB. granulated sugar

1 cup whipping cream

¼ tsp. vanilla

1 prepared 9-inch graham or cookie crumb
crust, or 9 phyllo cups (recipe follows)

Thinly sliced limes, cut into small wedges

In a food processor, or a large bowl using an electric mixer, cream together cream cheese, marmalade, and 2 tablespoons sugar until smooth. If not using a food processor, finely chop lime rind in marmalade into smaller pieces.

In a separate bowl, whip cream with the remaining 2 tablespoons sugar and the vanilla; fold half of whipped cream into cream-cheese mixture.

Spread cream-cheese mixture into prepared pie crust. Spread remaining whipped cream over top; garnish around edges with sliced lime wedges and chill. Or chill filling; then, when ready to serve, spoon into phyllo cups (recipe follows); spoon whipping cream on each, and garnish with fresh raspberries.

Phyllo Cups

6 sheets frozen phyllo pastry, thawed in refrigerator

Melted butter

Raspberries to garnish

Stack two sheets of phyllo pastry; brush top lightly with melted butter. Cut in half, lengthwise, then in three, crosswise. Place squares in six greased, large muffin cups. Repeat, placing a second double-layered square crosswise over each of the first squares. Repeat with two more sheets, this time using the six squares to make three more cups.

Bake on lower rack in a preheated 375°F oven for 6 minutes or until golden brown. Let cool. Fill just before serving.

Word to the Wise

Work quickly when using phyllo pastry as it dries out quickly. To keep pastry from drying out and cracking, cover with a slightly damp, clean tea towel.

Apricot Ladder Braid

This recipe is from Pat Moynihan-Morris, who teaches traditional bread-making and bread-machine courses. If you have a machine, just use any sweet dough (1½ pound) recipe from the bread-machine cookbook or manual.

Prep time: 35 minutes (does not include time for dough to rise) • Cook time: 20 to 25 minutes • Makes 2 loaves, about 10 slices each

Traditional Sweet Dough:

3 cups bread or all-purpose flour

¼ cup granulated sugar

2 tsp. quick-rise yeast

1 tsp. salt

1 cup milk

3 TB. softened butter or margarine

1 egg, beaten

Filling and Topping:

½ cup apricot jam

1 egg white

1 tsp. water

½ cup sliced almonds

Prepare sweet dough for the machine. Or use traditional method: In a large bowl combine flour, sugar, yeast, and salt. In a small saucepan over medium heat, heat together milk and butter until hot to the touch (125° to 130°F). Stir milk mixture into flour mixture; mix in egg. Knead together in a bowl until soft dough forms. Turn out on a floured board; knead until smooth and elastic, for 8 to 10 minutes. Cover dough and let rest for 10 minutes (this will make it easier to roll out).

Punch down dough (traditional or bread machine); knead for two to three minutes. Divide dough in two.

Roll half of dough out into 9×12-inch rectangle; spread ¼ cup jam lengthwise down center third. Make diagonal cuts one inch apart and three inches long from both sides. Beginning at one end, fold dough strips over jam (one side and then the other) overlapping in center. Pinch in ends to seal. Repeat with other half of dough.

Place braids on a greased baking sheet; cover with waxed paper and a light tea towel. Let rise for 30 to 35 minutes, until doubled, in warm area of kitchen.

Whisk together egg white and water; brush over top of braids. Sprinkle each with ¼ cup almonds. Bake in a preheated 375°F oven for 20 to 25 minutes or until golden brown. Cover loosely with foil if it browns too quickly.

 Word to the Wise

Use large eggs in recipes, unless otherwise specified. Recipes are developed using this size; larger or smaller eggs will add more or less liquid and throw off the recipe.

Fried Bananas Caribbean

Here's a quick dessert using the Caribbean Treasure Conserve or Piña Colada Jam. It's delicious served over vanilla ice cream or frozen yogurt.

Prep time: 15 minutes • Cook time: 4 to 6 minutes • Makes 2 servings

2 firm ripe bananas

1 TB. butter

½ cup Caribbean Treasure Conserve or Piña
Colada Jam

1 TB. amber or coconut rum, or water

Ice cream

2 TB. toasted slivered almonds

Fruitful Trivia

To toast nuts, spread out on a rimmed baking sheet; bake in 350°F oven, shaking occasionally, for 5 to 10 minutes, until they are lightly toasted and fragrant. Also try toasting them in a dry, nonstick skillet, stirring frequently until lightly browned.

Peel bananas; cut in half lengthwise and then into about two-inch pieces.

Melt butter in a large skillet over medium heat; place bananas cut-side down in the skillet. Reduce heat to medium-low and cook two to three minutes per side, until just tender.

In a small bowl, stir together conserve and rum. Pour over bananas and stir gently to coat. Cook just until heated through.

Spoon over ice cream and sprinkle with nuts.

Low-Fat Raspberry Mango Frozen Cake

This low-fat cake is easy to make, using frozen-fruit ices or frozen yogurt and low-fat pound cake. Mix and match flavors such as strawberry, orange, vanilla, lemon, lime, and so on. Use your favorite jam, mixed with a little liqueur if desired. Makes a terrific, cool birthday cake!

Prep time: 20 minutes • Chilling time: about 3 hours • Makes 8 servings

1 (10¾ oz.) pkg. frozen low-fat or fat-free
pound cake

⅓ cup raspberry or raspberry mango jam

2 cups mango fruit ice

2 cups raspberry fruit ice

Sliced mango, raspberries, or fruit mixed with
jam and liqueur, as toppings (optional)

Cut cake into slices about ⅝ inch thick. Line bottom of an eighth-inch springform pan with cake, trimming to fit, leaving no spaces; spread jam over cake.

Let mango fruit ice soften slightly at room temperature; transfer to a bowl and stir just until soft enough to spread. Spread evenly over jam; place in freezer for 10 minutes.

Meanwhile, soften raspberry fruit ice. Remove the pan from freezer; spread raspberry fruit ice over mango layer.

Cover with plastic wrap and freeze for about three hours or until firm. (Can be frozen for up to a month.)

To serve, remove the sides of the pan. Let cake warm slightly at room temperature. Slice into wedges using a sharp knife. Top with fruit if desired.

Variations

Try different flavors of *fruit ices* in this dessert, such as banana, mango and lemon (for three smaller layers), or strawberry and mango, strawberry and banana, etc., changing the jam that goes with it.

Well Defined _____

Fruit ices are frozen desserts made from puréed fruit or juice, water, and sugar. They are virtually fat-free. Fruit ices are similar to sorbets or sherbets (which may contain some milk products).

Vanilla Jelly Roll

Jams and jellies are great fillings for jelly rolls. Use almost any flavor of jam (raspberry mango, strawberry kiwi, blueberry orange amaretto) or red currant jelly to fill; dust with icing sugar, or ice with whipped cream.

Prep time: 20 minutes plus 15 minutes for assembly   •   Cook time: 15 to 20 minutes   •
Makes 8 to 10 servings

1 cup sifted cake and pastry flour

1 tsp. baking powder

¼ tsp. salt

4 eggs

1 cup granulated sugar

¼ cup water

1 tsp. vanilla

Icing sugar

1¼ cups jam or jelly

1 cup whipping cream

2 TB. granulated sugar

½ tsp. vanilla

In a medium bowl mix together flour, baking powder, and salt; set aside.

In a large bowl, with an electric mixer, beat eggs until thick and lemon colored, for about five minutes. Gradually beat in sugar until very thick. Beat in water and vanilla.

Fruitful Trivia

For the best flavor, use pure vanilla extract in recipes where the vanilla taste is key. It's worth spending a bit more on the good stuff!

Gently fold in flour mixture. Pour batter into 15×10-inch jelly roll pan that has been lined with waxed or parchment paper; spread evenly. Bake in a preheated 350°F oven for 15 to 20 minutes, or until cake springs back when lightly touched in center.

Cut along edges and turn out onto a clean tea towel that has been sprinkled lightly with icing sugar. Peel off paper; roll up while still warm in the towel. For jelly roll, roll up from short side; if using for trifle, roll up from longer side. Let rest until cool.

To fill, unroll cake, spread with jam, reroll, and trim end at angle to taper seam. Jelly roll may be prepared to this point and wrapped tightly with plastic wrap; and refrigerate for up to one day. Place on a platter with seam-side down. Dust with additional icing sugar or spread with whipped cream; whip cream with sugar and vanilla until stiff. Chill until serving.

Variation

Chocolate Jelly Roll: Substitute ½ cup sifted cocoa for the same amount of flour; spread with ginger pear with Crème de Cacao Jam or any cherry jam.

Sherry Trifle

This showy dessert is popular during the festive season. It is layered in a large glass bowl and can be made ahead. Make jelly roll using raspberry, strawberry, apricot, or red currant jams. Roll up from the longer side so that you get a long, thin roll.

Prep time: 40 minutes • Chilling time: 4 to 6 hours • Makes 8 to 12 servings

1 jam-filled vanilla jelly roll

¾ cup cream sherry

3 cups chilled custard (approximate), canned or homemade

3 cups mixed fruit such as raspberries, sliced strawberries, blueberries, chopped kiwis, mangoes, or mandarin oranges

1 cup whipped cream

2 TB. granulated sugar

½ tsp. vanilla

⅓ cup toasted slivered or sliced almonds

Slice jelly roll into ¾-inch slices; use about two thirds of cake to line inside and bottom of deep, straight-side glass bowl. Sprinkle with about ½ cup sherry; allow to soak into cake well.

Spoon half the fruit over bottom layer of cake; spoon half the custard over fruit.

Lay remaining jelly-roll slices flat over custard; sprinkle with remaining sherry. Add layer of remaining fruit and then custard.

Whip cream with sugar and vanilla until stiff. Spread over custard and chill for four to eight hours. Just before serving, sprinkle with nuts.

Well Defined

Trifle is a traditional English dessert consisting of a layer of sponge cake (or jam-filled jelly roll) doused with sherry or sweet wine, with a layer of custard placed over the cake, jam or fresh fruit and a layer of whipped cream. If you have a high, straight-side glass bowl or trifle dish, you might repeat the layers. Top may be garnished with additional fruit such as strawberries, raspberries, and sliced kiwifruit.

The Least You Need to Know

- A small amount of preserve can add a lot of flavor to desserts.
- Jams and jellies make terrific glazes when warmed and brushed over fruit tarts.
- Jams, jellies, or conserves are an instant filling for cakes, cookies, braided breads, and tarts.
- Preserves are a convenient ingredient to have on hand.

Notes

Notes

Chapter 13

Savories

In This Chapter

- ◆ Preserves used in savory recipes to enhance cheese, meats, and salads
- ◆ Learn about using herb, hot pepper, garlic, and wine jellies as flavoring agents

In this chapter, you will find some tasty recipes with preserves as the secret ingredient! Preserves make great ingredients and add a lot of flavor and interest to dishes. They add a touch of sweetness and fruit flavor, to complement cheese, meats, and vegetables. Savory jellies (herb, pepper, and wine jellies) can be added to sauces after deglazing and as part of a salad dressing. Use them to glaze meats near the end of cooking—chicken with apricot or mango, pork or ham with pineapple, lamb with rosemary jelly, etc. Use your imagination to jazz up your own savory recipes, too.

Baked Brie

This is a quick appetizer to make—warm oozing cheese with a topping: jam such as pears and Port or Peach Cranberry; conserve such as Fig and Italian Plum; chutney such as Apricot or Cran-Apple with Sage and Thyme. Or bake the Brie without removing the top, and serve with Red Currant or Fire-and-Ice Jelly.

Prep time: 10 minutes • Cook time: 10 to 12 minutes • Makes 6 appetizer servings

1 whole 4-inch round Brie, about 8 oz.

⅓ cup jam, conserve, or chutney

⅓ cup coarsely chopped pecans

Carefully cut top off Brie; this is best done while cold from refrigerator. Place in a shallow baking dish or foil-lined baking sheet.

Top with jam, conserve, or chutney; sprinkle with pecans.

Bake in a preheated 350°F oven for 10 to 12 minutes or until softened. Serve immediately with crackers.

Well Defined

Brie is a cream-colored soft cheese with an edible white crust or rind. It originated in the eighth century in France and is still made there, but good quality Brie is also made in the United States. **Camembert,** another soft cheese with a smooth, creamy interior, also originating in France, may be used in this recipe.

Coconut Shrimp

Here's a tasty appetizer to try. Warmed Piña Colada Jam makes the perfect dip for these scrumptious shrimp.

Prep time: 20 minutes (not including resting time)   •   Cook time: 25 to 30 minutes   •
Makes about 6 appetizer servings of about 6 shrimp each

1 egg yolk

½ cup milk

1 cup unsweetened shredded or medium desiccated coconut

½ cup all-purpose flour

½ tsp. salt

Pinch cayenne pepper

1 lb. large, uncooked shrimp, peeled and deveined (leave tails on)

Oil for frying

½ cup Piña Colada Jam (approx.)

In a small bowl, beat together egg yolk and milk. Stir in ¼ cup coconut, flour, salt, and cayenne. Cover and refrigerate for 30 minutes.

Prepare shrimp; dry well with paper towel. Cover and refrigerate until ready to cook.

Pour oil into skillet to about 1 inch deep. Heat over medium-high heat until it reaches 375°F.

Place remaining ¾ cup coconut in shallow bowl or on plate. Holding shrimp by the tail, dip into batter, then into coconut; shake off excess. Fry about 4 at a time in hot oil for about 30 seconds on each side or until golden brown. Remove with slotted spoon and drain on paper towels. Keep warm in oven.

Serve hot with Piña Colada Jam, warmed slightly in a small saucepan or microwave.

Word to the Wise
To "devein" a peeled shrimp, use a small, very sharp knife to cut a slit down the length of the back of the shrimp, revealing the grayish-black intestinal vein. Remove the vein using the point of the knife.

Purple Basil Salad Dressing

Use Purple Basil Wine Jelly to make this delicious vinaigrette to serve over mixed greens. Add sliced oranges or strawberries, thinly sliced red onion, toasted sliced almonds, or pecan pieces, and even edible flowers to your salad.

Prep time: 5 minutes • Makes 4 to 6 servings (½ cup)

3 TB. Purple Basil Wine Jelly

1 TB. white wine vinegar

1 tsp. Dijon mustard

Salt and pepper

¼ cup salad oil (not olive oil, as taste will overpower)

Mesclun mix salad greens

In a small bowl or glass measure, whisk together jelly, vinegar, mustard, salt, and pepper until smooth.

Slowly whisk in oil. Pour over mesclun salad just before serving.

Well Defined

Mesclun mix is an assortment of young greens such as: baby romaine, oak leaf lettuce, baby spinach, mizuma, curly endive (frisee), arugula, dandelion leaves, mache, radicchio, and so on.

Peach Barbecue Sauce

This tasty sauce is perfect for barbecued chicken or ribs. Also great on chicken wings—turn up the heat by adding hot pepper sauce to taste.

Prep time: 15 minutes   •   Marinating time: 3 hours   •   Makes 2⅔ cups

1 cup Peach Jam

1½ cups chili sauce (store-bought)

2 TB. vinegar

2 TB. Worcestershire sauce

1 tsp. ground ginger

½ tsp. garlic powder or 1 tsp. minced fresh garlic

Purée jam in a food processor or blender, or press through a sieve.

Add remaining ingredients to the food processor and blend until smooth in a medium bowl, or whisk together all ingredients.

Brush sauce over chicken or pre-boiled ribs and marinate for three hours. Brush additional sauce over top while barbecuing.

Fruitful Trivia

In place of chili sauce, you may use 1 cup drained diced tomatoes and ½ cup ketchup; add hot red chili pepper flakes (to taste) or chipotle chilis for a smokey flavor. Chipotles are dried smoked jalapeños.

Caribbean Chicken

Use Caribbean Treasure conserve or Piña Colada Jam to make this quick chicken dinner. Put some rice on first and it will all be ready in about 20 minutes.

Prep time: 20 minutes • Cook time: 20 to 25 minutes • Makes 4 servings

1 lb. boneless chicken breast

½ cup all-purpose flour

½ tsp. salt

Ground black pepper

1 egg, beaten

2 TB. oil

1 TB. cornstarch or all-purpose flour

1 cup chicken stock

½ cup Caribbean Treasure Conserve

Cut chicken into bite-size pieces. In a small bowl, mix together flour, salt, and a few grinds of pepper.

Dip chicken pieces into egg and then into flour mixture to coat.

In a large skillet over medium heat, heat oil. Cook chicken until golden; remove from the pan; set aside.

In a small bowl, whisk together cornstarch or flour and stock until well blended. Pour into the skillet and cook over medium heat until bubbling, scraping browned bits from bottom of pan. Stir in conserve until blended.

Return chicken to the pan, including any juice; cook for three to five minutes or until heated through and sauce is thickened. Serve over rice.

Fruitful Trivia

Allspice is the dried berries of the evergreen pimiento tree and is a typical seasoning of Caribbean dishes. Jamaica is the world's primary supplier. Used ground in sweet and savory dishes, it tastes like a blend of cinnamon, nutmeg, and cloves. It is used in the Caribbean Treasure Conserve. Add a pinch to this dish if using Piña Colada Jam.

Garlic Chicken Portobello

Garlic Jelly is a great ingredient to add to meat dishes for a touch of garlic.

Prep time: 15 minutes • Cook time: 20 to 25 minutes • Makes 4 servings

2 TB. oil, extra if needed

6 oz. *portobello mushrooms*, cut into ¼-inch slices

1 tsp. finely chopped fresh thyme, or ¼ tsp. dried

1 lb. boneless chicken breast

Salt and pepper to taste

½ cup white wine, chicken stock, or apple cider

3 TB. Garlic Jelly

¾ cup chicken stock

1 TB. all-purpose flour

2 TB. chopped fresh parsley

In a large skillet over medium heat, heat oil. Add mushrooms and thyme; sauté for three minutes or until softened. Remove from the pan; set aside.

Cut each chicken breast into two or three pieces; season with salt and pepper. Add a little more oil to the pan if needed. Place chicken in the pan and brown on each side; remove and set aside.

Whisk wine and jelly in a pan; cook over medium heat until bubbling, scraping browned bits from bottom of the pan. Whisk together chicken stock and flour; whisk into wine mixture. Cook for one or two minutes or until slightly thickened.

Well Defined

Portobello mushrooms are very large mushrooms with a dense meaty texture and rich flavor. They are the matured form of the brown-skinned cremini (or cremino) mushrooms.

Return mushrooms and chicken to the pan; stir in parsley. Cook over medium heat for three to five minutes or until heated through and sauce is thickened. Serve immediately. Serve with mashed potatoes or fettuccine, and baby carrots and broccoli.

The Least You Need to Know

- Preserves are useful ingredients that add flavor to many savory foods.
- Herbs, hot peppers, garlic, and wine jellies can be used as flavoring agents for glazes, dressings, and sauces.

Notes

Notes

Glossary

amaretto   An almond-flavor liqueur that is often made from the kernels of apricot pits.

boil   Gently boil—a steady boil that is not too vigorous, but is not as slow as simmering.

boiling water canner   A large pot with a rack, deep enough to process jars in boiling water with one- to two-inch coverage.

bubble remover   A long, thin, plastic tool used to remove bubbles from preserves after they have been ladled into jars.

canner   A large pot with a rack deep enough to process jars in boiling water with one- to two-inch coverage.

chili pepper   Crushed red chili-pepper flakes, dried chili peppers, and crushed chilies are all dried hot peppers. They are usually used in making hot pepper jelly and chutney in place of fresh chili peppers such as jalapeños.

chop   To cut into pieces, finely (about ¼ inch) or coarsely (¼ to ¾ inch).

chutneys   Tangy, sweet condiments of East Indian origin. They can range from mild to hot and are made from fruit and/or vegetables cooked with vinegar, sugar, and spices. Word originates from Hindi chatni, meaning "strongly spiced."

conserves   Jamlike preserves but with a thinner consistency than jams. They are typically made with two or more fruits, sugar, dried fruit, nuts, and sometimes liqueur. It should mound on a spoon.

cooking time   The estimated, overall cooking time. Begins from the point of turning the stove on, so includes heat up time for the pot and the contents. It includes the boiling or simmering time. It does not include resting time.

cream of coconut syrup   Available in most supermarkets near the canned-milk products or in specialty food stores. Do not confuse with coconut milk, which is not sweet.

crème de cacao   A clear chocolate-flavor liqueur.

dice   To cut evenly into cubes or pieces of about ½ inch or smaller.

fingertip tight   To tighten jar ring with just your fingertips gripping it; just until the ring is snug, but not as tight as it will go. Overtightening prevents air from escaping the jar during processing to provide a good seal. Also, tightening rings after processing is likely to disturb and weaken the seal.

freezer jam   A type of jam made without canning. Now called no-cook jam, as it can be frozen or stored in the refrigerator for up to three weeks. Freezing prevents microbial growth.

fruit butters   Smooth spreads made from puréed fruit, sugar, and sometimes spice; slowly cooked down to thicken naturally to a spreadable consistency.

full boil   A boil that cannot be stirred down, and that bubbles constantly and vigorously.

ginger   Crystallized and candied ginger are the same thing—ginger that has been preserved and is coated with granulated sugar. It is available in supermarkets and bulk stores, and comes in slices or pieces. Ginger root and fresh ginger are the same; the brown skin is peeled before using.

hard boil   A boil that cannot be stirred down, and that bubbles constantly and vigorously.

headspace   The space left between the surface of the preserve and the top rim of the jar. It is important to leave the required space to create the vacuum for a good seal. Jams, conserves, jellies, fruit butters, marmalades, and spreads are filled to within ¼ inch of the rim, while chutneys are filled to ½ inch of the rim. Contents from overfilled jars may seep out.

ice wine   A sweet, dessert wine made from grapes picked after they have been frozen on the vine.

jams   Spreads made from one or more fruits that has been crushed or chopped, combined with sugar or sugar substitute, cooked or uncooked. It gels from naturally present pectin or added commercial pectin, in combination with acid and sugar to become thick but with a soft, spreadable consistency. Jams should mound on the spoon.

jellies   Sparkling clear gels made with strained fruit juice (or other liquids, such as wine) and sugar; they are cooked, with or without added pectin, and they hold their shape but are tender enough to quiver and spread easily.

kirsch   A clear brandy distilled from cherry and juice and pits.

magnetic wand   A tool used for lifting prepared metal canning lids from hot water. It is a six-inch plastic wand with a magnet attached to one end.

marmalades   Fruit spreads made with one or more citrus fruits and other fruit or vegetable, using fruit pulp/juice and citrus rind that can vary from thickly cut to thinly shredded. It is set with naturally present pectin or added commercial pectin. Small pieces of citrus rind are suspended in a transparent jelly.

mince   To chop into very fine pieces.

pectin   A type of soluble fiber found in the skin, flesh, and seeds of fruit. Pectin, sugar, and high acidity are necessary for the gelling of preserves. Some fruit has suffi-cient pectin naturally present for a good set. Some may be low and require long boil-ing to concentrate the pectin. Commercial pectins are extracted from citrus fruit or apples and provide sufficient pectin to set without overcooking the fruit. *Do not* inter-change types of pectin (for example, liquid pectin for powdered pectin) in recipes or they will not work.

prep time   The estimated, overall time it takes to prepare ingredients. It includes the time to wash fruits or vegetables, all peeling, chopping, mincing, etc. to get them ready to add to the recipe. Also includes all measuring. Does not include any cooking time.

rapid boil   A steady boil that is bubbling well; a full rolling boil.

savory jellies   Sparkling clear gels made with wine, vinegar, juice, or water, and sugar; they are cooked, usually with added pectin, and they hold their shape but are tender enough to quiver and spread easily. They include hot pepper jellies, wine jel-lies, garlic jelly, and herb jellies.

setting point, set point, jelling point, gel point   The point at which your preserve is done, at which the sugar, pectin, and acid come together to create a gel and will set. There are various ways to test for it.

simmer   A constant, light bubbling over lower heat that slowly cooks the food.

spreads   Low-sugar or no-sugar (sugar substitute used) jamlike fruit.

yield   The approximate, minimal number of jars the recipe will make.

Appendix B

Resources

Ideas for Using Preserves

Here are some suggestions for using sweet preserves such as jams, jellies, conserves, and marmalades:

- ◆ Stir jams or conserves into plain or vanilla yogurt. Sprinkle with granola.

- ◆ Stir into cottage cheese (peach, apricot, berry preserves).

- ◆ Stir jams into cream cheese to spread on bagels.

- ◆ Stir a bit of jam into softened butter, add finely chopped dried cranberries and finely grated orange peel. Spread on hot scones.

- ◆ Place a spoonful of jam or conserve into center of muffin batter, top with batter, and bake. Or spoon bit of jam on top before baking.

- ◆ Add jam to pancake batter (strawberry, blueberry, cherry).

- ◆ Warm jams or jellies and drizzle over pancakes and waffles.

- ◆ Layer crêpes alternately with cream cheese and jam (strawberry, raspberry, cherry, apricot, and so on); stack crêpes, cut into wedges; serve with fresh strawberries, raspberries, blueberries, kiwifruit, and so on.

- ◆ Add preserves to breakfast shakes.

- Add a little jelly (raspberry, currant) to grapefruit halves and warm in a microwave.

- Use preserves to fill layer cakes or jelly rolls.

- Warm—with a little liqueur if desired—and brush over fruit flans or tarts to glaze.

- Use to fill mini tart shells (jams, conserve, or mincemeat).

- Swirl jam through batter for cheesecake before baking, or glaze cooled top with jelly.

- Make turnovers using jam inside puff-pastry triangles.

- Brush over roasted chicken or pork (herb or hot-pepper jellies) to glaze.

- Brush preserves over ham (pineapple, mango, or kiwi) to glaze.

- Brush on surface of squash halves before baking (apricot, pineapple, and so on).

- Stir a little jelly into cooked vegetables with a little butter (especially herb jellies).

Decorating Jars and Gift-Giving Ideas

It doesn't take much to turn your little jar of preserve into a presentable gift. Craft and fabric stores have lots of neat things you can use. Check out party packaging and stationery stores as well.

To decorate jars:

- Cut pieces of fabric (small prints of fruit or flowers, or seasonal prints) into five-inch circles using regular scissors, or using pinking shears to give a zigzag edge. Remove jar ring, place fabric over lid, screw jar lid back down (do not over-tighten). Wrap ribbon around jar ring and glue with hot-glue gun or tie into a bow. Or place the fabric over the jar ring, holding it in place with elastic; tie ribbon over elastic.

- Paper doilies can be used to top jars in place of fabric.

- Cut pieces of brown paper or tissue paper into 5-inch (12 cm) circles. Place under or on top of jar ring and tie with raffia or twine. Use rubber stamps to decorate brown paper or tissue paper with fruit, herb, or seasonal images. Stick gold or silver stars on paper, or draw with metallic ink pens.

- Tie small ornaments, small artificial fruit, dried flowers, or greenery such as ivy onto jars with ribbon or metallic string/rope, or hot-glue to jar ring.

- Hot-glue lace around jar ring; hot-glue small fabric rose where it meets.
- Print suggested uses for preserves on a tag; tie tag onto jar with ribbons or raffia.
- Use computer to print attractive labels.
- Use fancy wine bags available in liquor store or small gift bags; tie handles with ribbon.
- Package jars in a mini Christmas stocking or wrap several in tissue and place in larger stocking.

Ideas for gifts:

- Place a single jar in a small clear or decorated cello bag; tie with curling ribbon. Use stickers to decorate bags with seasonal (or other) theme. Inside the bag you could place an antique silver spoon or a spreader with a decorative handle.
- Use a small tray, basket, or cookie tin to hold a jar of preserves, fresh baked scones or muffins, small paper napkins, an antique silver spoon or jam pot/server with lid and serving spoon, and a small package of tea or flavored ground coffee.
- Things to add to gift baskets or bags might include small napkins, small knife and spoon (purchase in packages of four from gourmet kitchen stores or gift stores), or spreaders with decorative handles to fit theme.
- Bake a loaf of bread in your bread machine, place in basket lined with linen tea towel, and add jams, small cutting board, spreaders, napkins, and so on.
- With wine or pepper jellies, include cream cheese, box of crackers, bottle of wine, and pâté.
- With wine jelly or red currant jelly, include round of Brie or Camembert (especially attractive in round boxes with lids) or wafer crackers.
- With chutney, include small round of old cheddar cheese and crackers.
- Package small tub of spreadable cream cheese and fresh bagels with strawberry jam.
- Fill a basket with chutney, basmati rice, naan bread, and East Indian sauces such as korma or vindaloo (found in supermarkets); line basket with brightly colored East Indian fabric and add ornaments.
- For festive-season baskets, include cookie cutters, tree ornaments, bells, pine cones sprayed with gold, poinsettia napkins, or scented candles.

Resources and Fruit Websites

Alltrista Corporation

www.homecanning.com

Canning supplies, such as jars, lids, and rings (regular and decorative), magnetic wand (to lift lids from hot water), Ball Bubble FREER Spatula, jar lifters, labels, and so on.

Kraft Foods, Inc.

www.kraft.com

Click on "Contacts"; "For product and ingredient questions, as well as other consumer information, click here"; "Product Questions"; "Baking/Canning"; then "Sure-Jell Pectin." You'll find lists of answers to frequently asked questions or you can ask your own. Also available at 1-800-323-0768.

Here is a list of other websites you should check out:

◆ www.uscranberries.com

◆ www.kiwifruit.org

◆ www.concordgrape.org

◆ www.calstrawberry.com

◆ www.wildblueberries.com

◆ www.oregon-berries.com

◆ www.almanac.com/garden/saskatoon

◆ www.cherrymkt.org

◆ www.bestapples.com

◆ www.califapricot.com

◆ www.calraisins.org

◆ www.eatcaliforniafruit.com

For information on ordering organic dried lavender (for cooking) and other lavender products:

Purple Haze Lavender Ltd.

Sequim, WA

1-888-852-6560

www.purplehaze.com

Olympic Lavender
Sequim, WA
360-683-4475
www.olympiclavender.com

Lavender Green
Pennsylvania
www.lavendergreen.com

Index

W-X-Y-Z

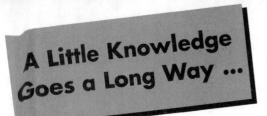
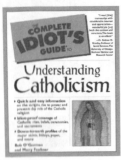

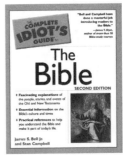

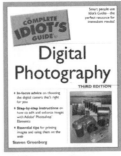